WRITING
BUSINESS LETTERS
AND MEMOS

The No Nonsense Library

NO NONSENSE REFERENCE GUIDE™

WRITING
BUSINESS LETTERS
AND MEMOS

Havis Dawson

To Liza,
who got the kids out of the house
so I could write this thing.

Copyright © 1993 by Longmeadow Press

Published by Longmeadow Press, 201 High Ridge Road, Stamford, CT 06904. All rights reserved. No part of this book may be reproduced or utilized in any form or by any means, electronic or mechanical, including photocopying, recording or by any information storage and retrieval system, without permission in writing from the Publisher.

Cover design by Kevin P. Oden

Interior design by Richard Oriolo

Library of Congress Cataloging-in-Publication Data

Dawson, Havis.
   Writing business letters and memos / Havis Dawson. — 1st ed.
    p. cm.
   ISBN 0-681-41682-3
   1. Commercial correspondence—Handbooks, manuals, etc.
2. Memorandums—Handbooks, manuals, etc. 3. Letter-writing-
-Handbooks, manuals, etc. I. Title.
HF5726.D318 1993
651.7′4—dc20   92-40326
                         CIP

Printed in United States of America

First Edition

0 9 8 7 6 5 4 3 2 1

Contents

Introduction

If you're among the increasing number of American workers who pursue their livelihood in the "service" sector—managers, salespeople, account executives, and clerks—good letters and memos can help you get more recognition, more satisfaction, and more money out of your working life.

Here's how to share your ideas so people want to read them—and act on them.

One

WHAT A BUSINESS LETTER OR MEMO SHOULD DO

A business letter or memo aims to:

- share information;
- encourage specific action; or
- create goodwill.

When you think about it, *every* project you do at your job falls into at least one of these three categories. A good letter or memo has a bit of all three.

Whether you're adding up quarterly sales figures or pitching a new piece of business over the phone, you're probably trying to *share information* ("Quarter sales were up"; "Our product has all the bells and whistles you want"). And, since any sales pitch should ask for the sale, you want to *encourage specific action* ("Let's aim even higher"; "You should buy now").

If you're lucky you'll also create *goodwill*—your tone will encourage the reader to enjoy working with you. Generally this goodwill is won through the tone of your letter, rather than through any outright statement (Not "I am a reasonable, hardworking guy"; or "You'll be happy you bought").

A concise letter with a clear point is one of the most cost-effective business tools at your disposal. The purpose of business writing, then, is just that: to do business.

What single guide best leads to a powerful, effective business letter? Simple: knowing what you want to say. If you keep in mind that goal and work to prune your presentation, you can write outstanding business letters.

Some people may feel a good idea will shine through even the most awkwardly constructed letter. Given enough time, perhaps. Alas, most readers can't devote the time to puzzle out the purpose buried under vague catchphrases and unclear sentiments. If we must sway our reader's opinion, we can't do it with arguments he can't follow.

The purpose of a letter is to enable the reader to hear your idea as you hear it in your own head. A letter aims to share your thoughts, not to obscure them through puffery or unnecessary formality.

Besides, a slim idea stretched into a bloated memo fools no one. Businesspeople are by training distrustful of the over-promise.

A well-phrased, well-typed letter that urges unsound action on illogical premises will soon be exposed if acted upon.

Yet a confusedly written letter that obscures its sound proposal may not even get read.

Present your ideas well. Get heard. And, we hope, get ahead.

FEAR OF WRITING

Why are many businesspeople intimidated by putting their thoughts onto paper? Let's look at some of the complaints.

- It's time-consuming. Yes, picking up the phone to exchange thoughts *is* faster than getting your thoughts onto paper in an attractive way and mailed off, only to await your target's reply. Most "active" business *is* best handled by telephone. But if you're trying to pitch a great many people at once, or if you need to lay out an important detailed scheme, the phone just won't do.
- I talk better than I write. Here's probably the greatest hurdle to good business writing—the feeling that talking is an intuitive, powerful link between people, while writing is a stiff and formal necessary evil. By this thinking, talking is heart-to-heart and writing is mind-to-mind, and a lot of us trust the depth of our hearts more than the subtlety of our minds. Too, business almost always relies on at least a dash of persuasion—the very stuff of talk.

And it's probably true: You probably *do* talk better than you write. Why shouldn't you? After all, you're well practiced at talking. You've learned to push the personal buttons of your listener.

Well, good writing is *personal* writing. And good writing is *persuasive* writing.

Aren't those the two qualities you value the most in your talk, too?

Maybe you just have an outmoded view of writing in general, and of business writing in particular.

Getting Free of Fear

Ask yourself: Why am I writing this letter? What do I want to tell the reader? What do I want him to do? Focus on the *purpose* of the letter. If you can do that, you can write good letters—letters that are probably better than the majority of letters that come across your desk every day.

Is that all there is to writing top-drawer letters? Of course not. But it's the core principle, the semipolished precious stone without which no jewel can be carved.

So get your "core" onto paper before you begin its polishing. Whether you're writing a two-paragraph memo or a ten-page proposal, begin with a first draft. Maybe your first draft will stand as your final version. Maybe you'll change the order and the wording of your letter until the final version is completely different from the first. Really, you just won't know until after you get started.

This awareness that you need not sit down and type out "the perfect letter" can be tremendously liberating. Don't wait until you know exactly what you want to say before you write it. That time will never come. Don't hesitate to change what you've written. That's how good writing gets even better—chopping away distractions and expanding on those points that hammer home your message. Just keep that message, that purpose, as your guiding star.

So get started.

There are as many ways to write a first draft as there are letter writers. You'll probably use different techniques for different projects. But there are two basic techniques:

- arrange notes, and
- just start writing.

NOTES

Obviously, the longer your letter the more it's likely to benefit from first writing out your notes. Only the unusually gifted among us can keep the structure of a multipage letter firmly in mind. But after you've purged your mind of the points you want to make by writing them down, and you see them all laid out alongside each other, then you can begin organizing them.

As with the letter itself, don't let structuring notes intimidate you. Trying to arrange your thoughts into a traditional rigid outline with roman numerals and capital and small letters can be counterproductive and frustrating. ("Let's see . . . would this be a new entry under subheading *c* or a new sub-subhead called *vii*?") If you can recognize the necessary "changeableness" of such an ostensibly "formal" outline, go ahead and use one. If not, instead try jotting down your main ideas and supporting examples onto a single piece of paper, using just a few key words to remind you of your thoughts. Some people find unlined paper is more conducive to free association.

Then, link the ideas and points that can be logically grouped together. Circle them and join them with arrows. Or number them similarly. Label your most important idea "Beginning." Label your second-most important idea "Ending." Arrange your other ideas between these two important anchors in descending order of importance, numbering then 1, 2, 3, and so on. If, when drafting your letter you decide an idea is more (or less) important than you first thought, simply move it.

JUST START WRITING

The just-start-writing method works best for shorter letters with a fairly simple purpose—a letter to accompany a requested item, for instance. It's also the usual method in writing a letter you write often. Here, you've written this type of letter often enough that you've got a good idea of what you want to say.

Basically, this is just a letter in which you keep your notes in your head, rather than writing them down. It doesn't mean you're doing some sort of "unconscious writing." Keep your purpose in writing firmly in mind as you build your argument.

Again, don't feel the just-start-writing letter has to be perfect right out of the box, either. Don't be afraid to let your thoughts take you down paths you haven't thought through. That's how you discover new ideas. And if you find yourself writing down a blind alley, just cross out the train of thought where it went off the track or onto a distracting soapbox.

TOOLS

You may write your letters with pen, pencil, typewriter, or word processor—it's up to you. Typed up on crisp bond, a letter originally drafted with crayon on a paper bag can be just as thoroughly professional as one drafted with all the RAM of IBM's hottest computer.

Even if you dictate your correspondence to a tape recorder or stenographer, you'll probably do your editing on paper. Dictation can be quick and easy (especially if you don't type), but it's sometimes difficult to construct a complicated argument into a seamless whole when you can't see your building blocks. Consider a long dictated letter a rough draft, then, and edit with an especially ruthless pen. (For tips on dictating and working with a secretary, see Chapter 15.)

You probably already have a way of working. If you're generally happy with it, I won't urge you to change. One key to good letters is comfort. If you've always written with black ink on ruled yellow pads, fine. If you've always banged your drafts out on a manual typewriter, more power to you. This book will help you get your thoughts in persuasive order, so you can do your job better. I won't presume to turn your working life upside-down.

Personally, I find that a word processor enables me to write more freely. Even if you're a two-finger typist—and a surprising number of professional writers are—a computer makes correcting typos or rearranging paragraphs or killing dead-end thoughts a snap. How many times have you noticed something you'd like to change in a letter just as you're about to sign it, but you let it go because you can't bring yourself to tear up the page and start again? All letters benefit from editing, and word processors make fine-tuning nearly painless.

The common wisdom, however, is that computers can make letter writing *too* easy, so that a simple note spins out into a four-page reflection encompassing any marginally related topic. Yes, this can be a danger for a facile typist. Still, I feel the advantage in putting on paper (or screen) all your thoughts on a subject before you cut will serve your writing better than limiting yourself because it's "too much trouble" to type them. Sometimes you discover your most critical points in letting your first draft wander a little bit. Just don't be reluctant to edit ruthlessly.

TIME (AND HOW TO USE IT)

Jotting notes, banging out stream-of-consciousness first drafts, editing down . . . it all sounds highly time-consuming. *Too* time-consuming for today's fast-paced, lean 'n' mean office pace, you may think. And unless the getting-started regimen I've described speeds your work right off the bat by eliminating time you formerly spent staring at blank pages awaiting inspiration, the first few times you try to craft a really good letter will take you longer than simply banging it out the way you used to.

But it's likely you're not fully satisfied with your current writing technique, or you wouldn't have picked up this book.

Like most things, writing business letters gets faster with time. The principles you practice will grow instinctual. You'll see earlier where you want to go with the letter you're putting together.

Here are some time-saving tips:

- Don't pad. Say what you want to say, then stop.
- Know why you're writing. *Express* your thought in your writing, don't *discover* it there.
- If you've written letters for similar purposes before, take a new look at them. Don't hesitate to "steal" sentences or paragraphs you've used before. If you hit on a felicitous way to describe your company or its products or its market, don't reinvent the wheel, borrow one. But don't torture an earlier use to make it fit a new need.
- Know yourself. Do you work better in the morning? With your feet on the desk and a pad on your lap? Don't think you have to work like everyone else.
- Know when to stop researching. Reading an entire file before moving forward is often a stalling technique. If you feel a guilty twinge that you're not getting started on a letter, put down the research and get started. Nothing helps you discover holes in your understanding like trying to formulate your argument.
- All tasks are not equally important. Restrict your greatest investment of time to letters of greatest importance: a critical sales pitch, contract negotiation, employment search, or maybe a memo to your boss.
- Know what you're trying to accomplish.
- Don't pad. (I say this again, for emphasis.)

No, good letters don't always come easy. But they can be easier with thoughtful practice. If you're among the increasing number of American workers who pursue their livelihood in the "service" sector—managers, salespeople, account executives, and clerks—good letters and memos can help you get more recognition, more satisfaction, more money from your working life.

A thing worth doing is worth doing well.

Two

THE TROUBLE WITH MOST BUSINESS LETTERS

The trouble with most business letters is, simply, *they're boring!*

They're boring, usually, for two separate—though often related—reasons.

1. Poor organization. If the reader can't readily follow your train of thought, he's going to hop off the track.
2. Business English. Would you choose to struggle through a letter in a foreign language you didn't really understand? Business English is a foreign language. I don't speak phrases like ''Enclosed herewith for your review and response,'' and I don't *think* in those phrases, either.

Happily, use of Business English has withered over the last fifty years. It's time to bury it completely.

Probably you don't use egregious examples of Business English. Probably you don't now write "Yours of the 15th in hand and contents duly noted" when you write Bob about his latest letter to you. Bravo.

But perhaps you haven't fully expunged your letters of phrases such as "Permit me to advise you that . . ." or "In re." These familiar Business English phrases don't particularly obscure your meaning, but they promote MEGO (My Eyes Glaze Over) in your reader.

These phrases are part of that great office tradition, jargon. Everybody uses these terms. Their appearance has the comfort of familiarity, and everybody "sort of" recognizes what the words mean. However, these words are at best space fillers that plump out a page while the letter reader wades on to reach your point. At worst, the use of this Business English obscures your point. For instance, just what *does* "Permit me to advise you that . . ." signal? Is the "advice" that follows mere background information or is it the crux of the letter's purpose? Is your intended tone that of humble entreaty or haughty condescension? That pat bit of jargon so often inserted at the beginning of business letters obscures your message, rather than moving toward it.

It's easy to fall into the habit of using jargon. These near-meaningless phrases are the written equivalent of spoken conversation's "hmmms" and "uhhhs." Your words are moving while you wait for your mind to catch up. This aspect of the habit is easy to avoid. Simply edit out these on-paper throat clearings if they find their way into your first draft.

But jargon has a darker side, too. Business jargon can obscure the fact that you're not thinking clearly. Enough professional-sounding jargon can "fuzz up" the fact that your insight is minimal or fractured. If your insight truly *is* minimal or fractured, and you've no intention of sharpening it, perhaps you *should* lard in all the jargon your slim argument can support. But beware, a close reader (such as someone who tries to base a decision on your provided information, or your boss) will quickly discern there is no emperor under the fancy dress.

Our tendency is to inflate the pomposity and length of our correspondence to sound more learned. Do yourself and your reader a favor: resist Business English.

Ask yourself:

- Have I said this as directly and clearly as possible?
- Would I say it this way if I were speaking?

Some businesspeople might say such conversational-style writing is too informal for his company or his position. I don't suggest your writing should read like a transcript of your weekend bull sessions. Instead, if you're writing to your corporate peers, write in the way you'd talk to them. If you're writing a letter or memo that will be read by businesspeople "above" you, write in the way you might talk to your boss.

SPEAKING VERSUS WRITING

So far, we have suggested that your writing should mimic your speaking—that your letters should present a casual, plain-talk tone. Can that be carried too far? Yes.

First, note that we suggest your writing should mimic thoughtful, articulate speech. Once uttered, a spoken phrase can never be fully retracted. The written word offers you the opportunity to fine-tune your expression. Use this freedom.

Conversation is by nature freewheeling, often repetitive. Thoughts often trail off or lead nowhere. If you've ever read an unedited transcript of conversations by even the most thoughtful of speakers, you'll find many sentences that spin on, double back, or peter out. In conversation, we filter this "noise" out of our comprehension of the speaker's point. The speaker's voice offers us clues in how to listen—what to ignore, when to perk up. Renewed enthusiasm after a period of flagging hesitancy in a speaker's voice tells us to ignore the dead end he just talked himself into and to pay fresh attention. These cues are absent, obviously, in written communication. Therefore, writing is more than simple transcription.

Also, listening is easier than reading. We are less demanding of strict logic and continual movement in our conversations than we are in our reading. The speaker who cuts himself short and announces, "Look, here's the point" is admired for his keen insight. However, we get annoyed with the writer who suddenly on page three stops to announce he's hit upon his theme. "Why didn't he say so before?" we fume.

It is expected that a letter sets out its argument logically, tersely. Who has time for less rigor?

The conversationalist is more readily forgiven, too, for overlong, complicated sentences and for abrupt sentence fragments. No reader likes long, confused sentences. Break a long sentence into two shorter ones. Don't make your reader look back for the subject of the sentence once he finally comes to the verb. Set off a descriptive qualifier—like this one right here—with dashes or commas. Never make the reader read a sentence twice to understand it. Most readers won't. Even those who take the trouble won't like being made to do so.

Sentence fragments (that is, sentences with no verbs) *can* be appropriate in written correspondence. Used wisely and sparingly, these punchy lines are powerful tools. Really. (That's a fragment.) Used indiscriminately, ultrashort sentences—and especially sentence fragments—halt the reader's flow and chop your letter into a series of seemingly unrelated bits. Also, unless you're highly confident about your writing, I'd advise against sentence fragments. Your reader might think you didn't realize you dropped the verb.

ACTION! WHO'S DOING THIS?

Use the "active"—not passive—voice. This is important, and it's easy to do. Don't let the techno-grammar term "active voice" put you off. An active-voice sentence is simply one in which the subject of the sentence performs the action named.

Active: I like chocolate.
Passive: Chocolate is liked by me.

Active: I'd like this report by Friday.
Passive: The receipt of this report by Friday is preferred.

Active: Our accounting office wants more information.
Passive: There is a request for more information from our accounting office.

The active voice tells the reader right away who is doing what. It keeps reader interest high. The active voice tells your story more clearly and more compellingly than the weaker passive voice. The active voice draws a picture in the reader's mind. He "sees" what's happening.

The passive voice fuzzes what's going on. It leaves a vague impression in the reader's mind, and his attention often wanders.

In my experience reading businesspeople's writing, the chief affliction is the pervasive, numbing passive voice. These people know their subject well. But following their train of thought through tortuous passive construction is often difficult.

I believe businesspeople think the passive voice sounds more official, more "professional" than the active voice, which carries the stigma of personal opinion. Don't be afraid to express your opinion. Probably you were hired to have one. Certainly that is why you are writing a letter or memo—to express *your* thoughts as a representative of your company. A personable letter is a letter that works.

The passive voice also reflects the basic way in which businesspeople learn to see actions. As a manager, business-people must take something of a god's-eye view: He tracks the completion of tasks or accomplishment of goals. That means he doesn't think, "Bob has cleaned valves one through eighteen," which is the active-voice way of phrasing the accomplishment. Instead, he thinks, "Valves one through eighteen have been cleaned," which is the passive-voice view.

This passive-voice view pervades his outlook. It is how the manager sees what has happened. And that viewpoint is deeply ingrained.

This manner of looking at things may help the manager keep track of what has been accomplished, but it makes for deadly dull reading for one simple reason: It doesn't draw a mental image of what is happening.

Let's look at two samples—one that describes the people and their activities and one that focuses on the task.

Task-centered Business English:
The maintenance of high quality standards is the goal established at the highest levels of management. Its accomplishment is pursued through continual feedback/review from the factory floor, particularly at locations along the conveyer line and the sanitizer.

People-centered Business English:
The general manager and other top managers set the goal of maintaining high standards. Factory floor personnel provide feedback and review from factory-floor activity—particularly at the conveyer line and the sanitizer.

The second example still sounds perfectly businesslike and professional, but it describes what the people are doing, not simply "what is being done" by unpictured actors.

Some businesspeople fear that in being urged to write in the active voice using an actor-centered viewpoint, they are being urged to write "touchy-feely happy-talk." As you see from the example above, this isn't necessarily so. Happy-talk—a term that's not necessarily derisive—can very effectively describe your thoughts in a way even the unitiated reader can follow.

Businesslike happy-talk:
The general manager and other top managers urge us to maintain high quality. We do that by continually checking with

the people who work on the factory floor—especially those who know about the conveyer line and the sanitizer.

Happy-talk can, of course, be taken too far.

Questionable happy-talk:
The boss and other front-office guys urge us to keep quality high. We do that by staying in touch with the people on the factory floor, especially those who know about the conveyer line and the sanitizer.

You must find a tone that is appropriate for your audience. You don't want to sound flippant in trying to sound approachable. But no matter how formal you feel you must be in your presentation, you need not write bureaucratic Business English. If you're reluctant to drop the unseen-actor, task-centered style of presenting your information because you fear it will look insufficiently professional, consider this: A clear, readily grasped description of the situation lets the reader know *you* have a clear and ready grasp of the situation. A complex, convoluted description reinforces the notion in the reader's mind that you are nearly overwhelmed with the situation.

An active-voice description of a situation is simply easier for a reader to follow.

Sometimes, though, you may *want* to use the passive voice, to draw attention away from the actor and to focus attention instead on the action itself. Most often, you'll use this technique when sharing bad news.

Passive: Your request is denied.
Active: I deny your request.

Passive: Mistakes were made.
Active: I was wrong.

Try to reserve the passive voice for such special occasions.

Do you want your business letters to be faceless, blameless, boring texts like deeds, wills, and tax regulations? I think not.

Put the people in them, then.

Business writing takes place not between corporate entities but between people. Business communication—at all levels, among clerks and among CEOs—is a person-to-person meeting of minds, not an Inc.-to-Inc. meeting of balance sheets.

The active voice *is* a professional tone. It accepts and assigns responsibility. It speaks clearly and compellingly. It *works*.

Don't imagine your reader won't recognize good writing. He may not be able to label its parts, but he'll read and understand it and—the greatest test—perhaps be moved to action by it.

The passive voice sneaks into all writing. You need constant vigilance to knock it out of your letters and memos.

ACTION! GIVE IT PUNCH

We just discussed the value of using the active voice—we put the actor into the sentence. Now let's look at the value of using an action verb—let's smack the player bang into there.

Look back at the paragraph above. "We put" is an active-voice sentence with a rather weak verb, *put* "Let's smack" though, is an active-voice sentence with an action verb, *smack*. See the difference?

Choosing what is and what isn't an action verb is a matter of opinion, since the level of action implied is a matter of degree. Is *put* an action verb? Probably not. Is *smacked?* I'd say yes. Is *insert?* Maybe.

Deft handling of action verbs requires an accomplished ear. The temptation is to edit every verb into its "punchiest" counterpart. Suddenly, we never simply exceed our quotas: We nail them; we explode them; we blast past them. Two problems with this tendency: All actions sound equally important, and they all begin to sound rather juvenile.

There is a middle ground. Look first to replace any verbs

that describe simply a state of being; these are notoriously weak verbs:

Weak: A state of emergency exists in the boiler room.
Descriptive: The boiler has burst.

Weak: Sales are at a new high.
Descriptive: Sales have hit a new high.

Weak: Fear prevailed in the boardroom.
Descriptive: Fear hovered in the boardroom.
Even better (though probably not professional): The directors twitched with fear.

But be careful not to exaggerate the effect to an inappropriate level.

Exaggerated:
The boiler blew to smithereens.
Sales zoomed to a glorious new high.
Fear thundered through the boardroom.

WORDINESS

*"I hope you will pardon me for writing such a long
letter, but I did not have time to write you a shorter one."*
—Blaise Pascal, 1623–62
(French mathematician and philosopher)

Don't be embarrassed to write a wordy sentence. Be embarrassed only if you mail one.

That means editing.

Sometimes our thoughts are so filled with particulars that our sentences are confusingly over-stuffed. Instead of describing the forest, we detail the trees. At editing, then, the trick is to recognize when we serve the reader by changing "three 20-foot birch trees, fourteen 35- to 45-foot maples, fifteen to twenty 40-foot-plus oaks, and a smattering of walnuts" to "mixed hardwood forest."

Wordiness stems from two causes:

- trying to tell everything you know, and
- Business English.

Wordy: I should like to request that our Dallas office review this agreement with the aim of considering it for possible approval.
Straightforward: I'll ask our Dallas office to review this agreement.

Don't try to list every possible alternative action. This urge to cover all bases probably stems from our exposure to those most official of documents, legal documents.

Repetitive: Please review, note, mark, and revise any problems, inconsistencies, difficulties, or concerns.
Clear: Please mark your questions or suggestions.

AVOID CLICHÉS

Certain phrases are repeatedly found in most business letters and memos. These clichés make writing easier. Sometimes they boost reader understanding by pitching an idea in a recognizable phrase. Too often, though, a cliché's overuse has weakened its impact. Also, these ready-made phrases are by their nature rather general and vague, so clichés can be plugged into any number of needs, weakening their particularness.

When possible, change a cliché into an expression specific to your letter, to drive home your point more specifically.

This is particularly appropriate when the cliché phrase is your final, "take-away" sentence.

Cliché: Your cooperation in this distressing matter is appreciated.
Specific: Please tell Bob he's fired.

Clichés and jargon often sneak into first drafts. There's little shame in this. Your thoughts are still forming. Shame falls only on the writer who doesn't edit away clichés and jargon.

Using the Thesaurus

A thesaurus offers you alternative words to express your thoughts. Because we're more familiar with using a dictionary than a thesaurus we may thoughtlessly assume that the words that follow a thesaurus entry—like those that follow a dictionary entry—*define* that entry word. They don't. The thesaurus groups words that are similar, though not neccessarily identical.

Don't go to a thesaurus to learn new words. Go there to remind yourself of words you already know well.

If you select from a thesaurus a word you "kind of" know, you risk looking foolish to a reader more familiar with it, who might recognize its inappropriateness. Worse, you may say something you don't mean at all.

To get a sense of how different are the meanings of words grouped in a thesaurus, look up a simple, everyday word. Like *big*. There you'll find everything from *gargantuan* (with its implications of power and strength) to *obese* (implications of fat), from *grand* to *gross*. Obviously, the images of these word choices are quite different. Choose with care. One reason English offers so many choices of words is that subtle differences of meaning exist among them.

And certainly I recommend against hunting the thesaurus for words to impress. This habit strikes a body blow against natural-sounding writing. Words plucked from a book and inserted into a letter usually look it. The "foreign" word jumps out at the reader.

Trust your own words. Don't go out of your own style to embellish or impress.

Three

LAYOUT AND
PAGE MECHANICS

Would you show up for an important business meeting dressed in a torn T-shirt and dirty shorts? Of course not. Likely no one would take you seriously. Perhaps some people would look past your appearance to hear your ideas. But most wouldn't bother. Instead, they'd interpret your slovenliness as disinterest and disorganization. You've lost them before you open your mouth.

Well, your business letter represents *you* at the meeting that takes place on its recipient's desk.

The first impression a reader gets of your letter is its appearance. The paragraphs' placement on the page, the typesize, the typeface, the letterhead, the quality of paper: That piece of paper is you.

Studies show that we form our impression of someone within the first few seconds of meeting. These first impressions are hard to shake. Make a good first impression with your letter. Make it easy for the reader to get to know you.

Lay out your letter, then, balanced on the page, in a format the reader recognizes as being professional. Simply, the *format* of the letter should not detract from the *content* of the letter.

Later in this chapter we'll discuss the appropriateness of departing from traditional business letter formats, by using headlines or different-sized typefaces. The advent of computers has made such tweaking temptingly simple, but too often such tricks are merely distracting.

In the great majority of cases you'll want your business letter to look like just that: a business letter. This means putting type where the reader expects type and white space where the reader expects white space.

Leave lots of white space. This keeps your page friendly on the eyes and invites the reader to dip into it. Most writers err on the side of too much type rather than too much "air." Densely typed letters, like densely written ones, too often go unread. They simply look like too much work to wade into.

Like a handsome tool, a balanced page layout invites use. A letter that begins and ends too high up on the page looks awkwardly top-heavy. One that runs low also looks poorly planned. These skewed layouts convey a simple message: "I didn't care enough about this letter to make it look nice." Your reader will be tugged by a similarly simple urge: "Then it must not be important enough for me to read carefully."

Your business letter is a business meeting carried out by mail. If you attended a meeting with your hair in disarray and your shirttail hanging out, your appointment would doubt both your interest and your judgment.

Your letter's appearance is equally important. If the writer didn't care enough to lay the page out gracefully, runs the reader's subconscious, its contents must not warrant my careful attention.

Don't be afraid to ask your typist—if you're not typing your letters yourself—to adjust his or her standards to fit yours.

Unfortunately, it's not always easy to estimate where a letter will end when you begin typing it. Experience and guesswork play almost equal roles. It's painfully time-consuming to tear up an otherwise perfect letter simply because it sits on the page awkwardly. Even when you're using a computer and can readily spit out a new version at the push of button, it's not always easy to justify the time pursuing such a nuance. Rejecting a letter as "unaesthetic" is no science; ultimately your "feel" is the final arbiter. Like your choice of tie or your hairstyle, some choices are yours alone.

PAPER

The traditional letter size is, of course, 8½ by 11 inches. (In the United States and Canada. English and Continental forms are longer.) This size page is always appropriate, no matter how long or short your letter.

However, if you want to "dash off" a quick note, particularly a handwritten one, smaller note-sized pages are perfectly appropriate. A 6-by-9-inch notepad of heavyweight paper headed by your company logo, your name, and title offers a convenient alternative to formal letterhead.

White bond paper, too, is the always appropriate medium. Colored paper—even so subtle a shade as gray or "oatmeal"—may distract from the forthrightness of your message. Appropriate bond is generally 25 percent rag content, and at least 20- or 24-pound weight. A paper weight higher than about 32 pounds is probably distractingly luxurious, at least in 8½ by 11 format. Note-sized paper benefits from a heavy weight; a weight sufficiently crisp in full-sized paper may seem inappropriately "casual" in notepad size.

If your firm provides letterhead paper (most do), use it for your first page only. Use blank bond for the following pages.

(A very few firms provide "following page" letterhead, with a discreet company logo. If available, by all means use this nice resource.)

Do *not* number your first page of a multipage letter. If you want to number the pages on a long letter, begin any numbering with the second page. A letter of three or fewer pages probably need not be numbered. A letter of four or more pages would probably benefit from numbering, as it eases reshuffling should the pages get misordered.

Use Arabic numerals (1, 2, etc.), *not* Roman numerals (I, II or i, ii, etc.). Numbers are placed either at the top center or top right-hand corner, or at bottom center. Hyphens may bracket any centered numbers, if you feel that otherwise the numbers look a bit lonely there.

A one- or two-word descriptive of the letter—usually the name of its receiver or, more rarely, its subject—may also accompany the page numbers, if you like. Usages such as:

Mr. Smith: 2

or

Page 2

XYZ consolidation

may ease confusion in later collating the letter's pages or might remind the reader of a long letter of its aim. But, to this writer, such aids seems unnecessarily ambitious.

If you are sending a memo or a fax, and your company provides pertinent memo or fax forms, by all means use them. Such visual cues help the reader immediately grasp what he has in hand. We'll discuss these types of communications within their own chapters later in this book.

TYPEFACE

Replaceable-ball typewriters, such as the tanklike, ubiquitous IBM (now Lexmark) Selectric, first lent letter writers a degree of flexibility in the size and style of typeface in which they chose to type their work. Word processors broadened that flexibility to horizons ball bangers never dreamed of. Well, dreams are distracting. Keep it traditional.

Typefaces can generally be divided into two broad groups: serif and sans serif. A serif is any one of the little lines that angle off the main strokes of a letter—the horizontal lines that "finish off" the letters. A serif typeface is one that uses these little lines in the design of its letters. A sans serif type has no little-line "decoration" (*sans* means "without" in French). Sans serif typefaces are generally simpler than serif typefaces, but serif typefaces are more traditional.

Stick with tradition is my advice.

Most sans serif typefaces are too "casual" for business letters. Also, they are simply unexpected in a business letter and may distract from your message.

The standard typesize for letters is 10 points. A slightly larger size, 12 points, is also acceptable. I suggest going no smaller than 10 and no larger than 12.

Many word processors can change typeface and typesize simply and easily—even within the same document. In general, my advice is: Resist. Stick with a single typeface in a single typesize for the entire letter. Mixing types within a letter—bigger and bolder for key items, for instance—looks just too complicated. It makes your business letter look like a handbill for cut-rate retail goods. ("One flight up! Bargains! No refunds!")

The only exception I would offer to this admonition against mixing type is their use to give memos a heading. If practice within your company is to produce memos with word processors, you may choose to head them MEMO in a large type of any pleasant style. But if everyone else uses company memo paper, you use it, too. Again, don't let your medium distract from your message.

Smudges and Corrections

Continuing the analogy of your letter page as your business face, keep your letters clean.

If your typewriter keys or type ball is dirty, clean it. Don't let people say, "Oh, here's another letter from Bob. I recognize the filled-in circles of the 'e's."

If you spill coffee along its edge, drop a dot of mustard in the margin, or stamp an inky thumbprint alongside the date, consider redoing the letter. Would you go to a meeting with coffee on your shirt, mustard on your tie, or ink on your nose?

Typos, typos, typos. Did you leave out a word? Misspell one? If it's on the computer, no problem: Edit and hit P for print. But if it's from the typewriter, you must decide: When is it worth doing over? Only you can say.

Spacing on the Page

The artful business letter provides sufficient "breathing-room" margin around the text. Leave around 20 letter spaces, about 1¼ inches, of left-hand margin. A bit more is better than a bit less.

Your right-hand margin should allow at least 1¼ inches of space, too. Obviously, some sentences will run longer to the right than others (unless your computer justifies—that is, stretches and squeezes lines to fit flush left and right—which I feel is inappropriately formal and machinelike, and also makes for some rhythm-wrecking stretched spaces). But to the reader's eye, your right-hand margin is defined by the longest one or two sentences on the page. One overlong sentence redefines the right-hand margin on a page. So set your margin tab to give you sufficient warning that you can avoid both awkward word breaks and awkwardly long lines.

In general, never break a word so that you leave a one- or two-letter "widow" on the last line of a paragraph. And if you have any doubt of where a word is properly broken, look it up.

The date is the topmost typed line of the traditional business letter. Since the rest of the letter's elements will fall into place based on that of the date, its placement will directly affect whether the letter falls well spaced on the page. Depending on the size and type of letterhead you use, leave about an inch of space between the bottommost part of the letterhead and the date.

The final line of the letter should be no closer than 1¼ inches from the bottom of the page. Obviously, it's difficult to plan just where the final line will fall. You can "cheat" the spacing a little by allowing more or fewer line spaces for your signature. And though purists may shake their heads at the suggestion, I propose you may elect to add line spaces between the body text and the complimentary closing to stretch to fill the page appropriately.

Sender's Heading and Date

The topmost line of a letter is the date. If you aren't writing on letterhead paper, you may wish to incorporate the date into the final line of your sender's heading:

XYZ Corporation
Boston, MA 02130
January 1, 1993

Many stylists advise writers to spell out all words in the company name, including Incorporated, Company, and so on. My advice for company names here and in the inside address is less hidebound: Abbreviate common terms if you like, as long as their meaning is readily recognized. That means Inc., Co., Div., Ltd., and Corp. are just fine. Avoid abbreviations such as A/C (for Air Conditioning), Trkg. (for Trucking), Publ. (for Publishing) and the like, though.

Since the U.S. Post Office encourages letter writers to use the two-digit state code on the outer envelope, for consistency you should use the system on the letter itself, as well. If you're at all unsure about the abbreviations, look them up. Most problematic: ME (Maine), MA (Massachussetts), MO (Missouri), MS (Mississippi), and MI (Michigan).

Spell out the month; don't abbreviate it and don't use numerals (e.g., 1/10/93).

PAGE LAYOUT AND INDENTATION

There are three standard page layouts for business letters. Each follows block form, which means each letter element (date, inside address, salutation, each paragraph, closing) is separated from one another with a line space. The three forms vary only in their use of indentation.

Probably this aspect of business letters is the bit of discipline you remember most vividly from those high school English classes: all those pages of letter layouts from John Smith of the ABC Corporation acknowledging to Bob Jones of XYZ Inc. his receipt of 100 widgets. You counted the line spaces between the date and the inside address, between inside address and salutation. You monitored your lines as they approached the right-hand margin, gauging when to break a word. Probably you thought it foolish.

Foolish or not, you learned it. You internalized it. Now those guidelines define how you expect a business letter to look. That's fine. In fact, it's to the good because it makes deciding how to lay out your letter much simpler. Layout rules do what the best rules do: They make life simpler by narrowing your choices.

Still, choices exist.

Let's look at the three traditional layouts you may choose among.

BUSINESS BLOCK

This is the traditional business letter layout. We say traditional, though in fact it has found widespread acceptance only this century.

In all block forms, one line space is left between each letter element and between each paragraph.

In personal writing and in most published works (including this book), paragraphs run "closed" to one another, with each first line indented. This closed format underscores the fact that this writing has a more overriding narrative purpose than does most business writing. In other words, nonbusiness writing tells a story; business writing sets out a stepwise argument.

The block form aids quick reading. It allows the reader to visually single out any one (or more) paragraphs in whose contents he is most interested.

Again, the three types of popular block forms vary only in their indentation.

The *business block* form indents the date, the close, and the signature to a far-right margin, while the inside address, salutation, and body are flush left.

January 1, 1993

Mr. Bob Jones
Vice President, Sales
XYZ Corporation
123 Main Street
New York, NY 10010

Dear Mr. Jones:

This is an example of business block formatting. As you can see, all elements except the date, the close, and the signature are flush left on the page.

This is probably the most common format used in business today.

It has in great part supplanted the more traditional semi-block style, with its indented first line of each paragraph—though the business block format is probably losing ground to an even simpler format, the full block format.

Sincerely,

Jim Smith
Marketing Director

JS:bt

The *semiblock format* is just like the business block format, except that the first line of each paragraph is indented.

January 1, 1993

Mr. Bob Jones
Vice President, Sales
XYZ Corporation
123 Main Street
New York, NY 10010

Dear Mr. Jones:

This is an example of semiblock formatting. As you can see, it varies from the business block style only in that each paragraph's first line is indented.

Many writers prefer the semiblock format because its indentation evokes the look of private correspondence. Other writers consider its indentations superfluous since each paragraph is separated from the other with a line space, giving the reader all the visual cues he needs.

Semiblock format could be considered more old-fashioned than business block or full block style, but its use is perfectly acceptable.

Sincerely,

Jim Smith
Marketing Director

JS:bt

The *full block* format contains no indentations. All elements are typed flush left.

January 1, 1993

Mr. Bob Jones
Vice President, Sales
XYZ Corporation
123 Main Street
New York, NY 10010

Dear Mr. Jones:

This is an example of full block formatting. All elements of the letter are flush with the left margin. There are no indentations.

The full block format is probably the easiest of these three formats to type. However, some writers consider it a bit too efficient-looking, a bit too machinelike.

However, the full block format business letter is probably the fastest-growing style. It will probably someday sup-

plant business block as the format used most, though business writing is notoriously slow to change.

Sincerely,

Jim Smith
Marketing Director

JS:bt

These are the three most common formats for business letters. There are, however, a number of writers who see too much wasted time and space in these formats and urge adoption of a simpler, more streamlined format. Specifically, these writers suggest dropping the salutation and the complimentary close. Other alterations, such as banner first line as might be found in a memo, are also proposed.

January 1, 1993

Mr. Bob Jones
Vice President, Sales
XYZ Corporation
123 Main Street
New York, NY 10010

THIS IS AN EXAMPLE OF A QUASI-MEMO LETTER.

All elements are flush with the left margin. No salutation or complimentary close is inserted. Both are considered unnecessary.

The aim of this type format is simplification. Certainly getting rid of the salutation erases one sometimes difficult political decision: how to address your reader.

Is Mr. Jones too formal? Is Bob overly familiar? If you've never spoken with someone named Chris or Terry, do you salute them Mr. or Ms.?

And what's the point of the complimentary close, anyway? How many writers actually vary their complimentary closing to reflect the circumstances, choosing among Sincerely or Most Sincerely or Sincerely Yours? Very few.

The logic and efficiency of the simplified form is evident—but not, I believe, compelling. I think most businesspeople find it off-puttingly abrupt. Such personable though unnecessary touches as the salutation and the complimentary close will not die away soon, I believe.

Jim Smith
Marketing Director

Four

INCORPORATING PROPER GRAMMAR AND SPELLING

Everybody grew up hating the rules of grammar and spelling. But these rules offer reassurance. In a world in which almost nothing is forbidden and everything is open to negotiation, it's nice to find a firm set of guidelines.

Grammar books and dictionaries set forth what is "preferred" usage. Preferred by whom? By the book's writers and editors, of course. More than simple personal preference, though, these writers peg proper use to the grammatical equivalent of law's "reasonable (wo)man," sometimes called the thoughtful speaker or the educated writer or some such *nom de grammar*. This imaginary thoughtful writer is aware of the word and grammar choices that the English language presents her, and she selects one she hopes will express herself most perfectly and with the least jar on the ears of a similarly discriminating audience.

Grammatical rules help you to write in such a way that the substance of your letter is not overshadowed by constructions that distract the reader.

Sometimes, you may consciously choose to "break" a rule—in humor because you feel the rule is foolish and antiquated. The best guideline for when to break a rule is: Be sure your reader *knows* you know better.

We won't attempt here to dissect all the rules of grammar and writing. That's a much thicker book than this unto itself, and you should keep one or two such books available to you where you work, such as Strunk and White's *The Elements of Style*. Here we'll just look at some of what my experience tells me are the most oft-broken rules in business writing, and some for which general grammar books offer too little advice.

CAPITALIZATION

If I could offer only one bit of guidance to aid the business writer hesitant over whether to capitalize a word or not, I'd simply say: When in doubt, lowercase.

Unneeded, excessive capitalization makes a letter look a bit like a bush in need of trimming. All those caps jump out at the reader and, by calling attention to themselves, distract the reader from what you're saying. Also, they distract the discriminating reader simply because he knows they're wrong.

Here are some guidelines:

- Capitalize only proper nouns, not common nouns. A proper noun is the name of a *specific* person, place, or thing:

  That's Doctor Kildare.
  Take a left on Main Street.
  We vacation on Lake Superior.

A common noun can refer to any one of two or more persons, places, or things:

The doctors agree.

High Street is the main street.

In its clarity, Lake Geneva is a superior lake.

• Do not capitalize simple for emphasis.

This is probably the greatest misuse of capitalization in business letters. Many writers feel the urge to capitalize words they feel are important. This is not sufficient reason and, rather than emphasizing the importance of the sentiments, such arbitrary capitalization merely distracts the reader from it.

For instance, I can readily imagine getting a letter or an internal memo in which I am told:

It is Company Policy to capitalize words that somehow seem like they are titles. And as long I am running the Company, that practice remains fixed.

Why is *Company* so often capitalized in business correspondence, particularly when referring in-house to one's own company? I think it may have something to do with analogy of the company to one's mother. Don't laugh. After all, we capitalize Mother (and Father and God) when we use the words as names, though we lowercase them when they're merely descriptive, for example:

I've often asked Mother if she is truly the best mother in the world.

Or perhaps Company is considered a shortened form of the company's name. Or, more likely, there's no hard logic running through the practice. The writer simply wants you to know he regards his firm with utmost personal gravity.

By the rules of grammar, ''company'' should not be capitalized. However, if everyone else in your firm capitalizes the word—like some sort of talismanic invocation—and you risk the squiggle-eye by lowercasing it, by all means capitalize your Company. Just try to keep the habit from spreading to other just-as-important nouns in your sentences. Like Fiscal Year. Or Annual Report.

Words listed in series often suffer the indignity of unnecessary capitalization, too, at the hands of undiscriminating writers:

The product is: Water, Sugar, Citric Acid, Sodium Benzoate, etc.

If you can't cite the rule or logic that drives your urge to capitalize a particular word, doubt its appropriateness. Then, look it up or ask someone around the office whose opinion on such matters you value.

- Capitalize titles only when they are used as part of the person's name:

    My dad once golfed with President Eisenhower.
    The president at the time, Eisenhower, once golfed with Dad.

This rule is simple to apply with one-word titles, and the grammar rule books are filled with readily grasped examples such as Bishop Orphrey, General Powell, or Senator Claghorn. Business titles are rarely so short and snappy, however. It's often difficult to gauge whether a long title is used as *part* of someone's name or as simply a preceding *descriptive* of his name. When you use his title *after* his name, its use as a descriptive rather than as a part of his name is obvious:

Bob Jones, vice president of marketing, will visit the plant.

But what about when you use his title right before his name? Is it:

We enjoyed the visit by vice president of marketing Bob Jones.

Or is it:

We enjoyed the visit by Vice President of Marketing Bob Jones.

Can we really say that titles like this are used as a part of someone's name, in the same way as, say, General Robert E. Lee's title is part of his? I don't think so. Therefore, I suggest we assume such a title is used as a description of the person rather than as part of his name. (I must confess that two other, not wholly legitimate, impulses also urge me to come down on the lowercase side of the question. First, I feel that excessive capitalization is a mark of unsophistication. Unaccomplished writers, eager to lend their words greater emphasis than their vocabulary allows, will too often capitalize any they feel are Important, with little Regard for Rules or consistency. Second, in capitalizing long titles the reader—and the writer—loses sight of the human being behind the title.)

Why do some writers like to capitalize all titles? Well, the practice does make the title look ominously important and, more specifically, it points out to the reader that the words are an official, company-sanctioned title, not just your description of his duties. These are honorable impulses.

If you insist, you may capitalize such a title before someone's name and insist it is part of his name. Just don't expect *me* to buy it.

A similar dilemma hangs over the capitalization of a corporate department or division. Are you in the mortgage division or the Mortgage Division? Is he in the maintenance department or the Maintenance Department? Here we have a bit more clear-cut guidance from traditional grammars. Go ahead and capitalize the group's name if it's recognized within the company by that name. Most of the time you're probably using such an officially sanctioned proper name: Sales and Marketing Department, Specialty Chemicals Division, etc. Certain names, though, may be chiefly descriptive and may be missing from any job roster at headquarters. These names are lowercased: headquarters, residential sales office, planning department, etc.

ABBREVIATIONS

In deciding whether to abbreviate a word or to spell it out, the rule of thumb is to choose the one that reads most easily—the use that the reader most expects to see. For instance:

I live on 52nd Street.
not
I live on 52 St. (The eye clunks on the telegraphic style.)
or
I live on Fifty-Second Street. (Not bad, and preferred by some, but the spelling out of the numbered street's name seems unexpectedly florid to me.)

Abbreviate *Incorporated*, *Corporation*, *Limited*, and the like, unless the word seems an integral part of the company's identity. The same guideline holds for *Company*, but that word probably falls more often under the "integral part" label.

Amalgamated Printing and Pressing Inc.
Worldwide Processing Corp.
Three Brothers Ltd.
Beanie Weanie Heavy Equipment Co.
but
Shirts Incorporated
The Bangor Corporation
Weinie Company
and certainly
Incorporated Inkwell Testers
Corporation for Public Broadcasting

(Note the absence of a comma before Inc. And Corp. In continuing pursuit of lean, mean "current as tomorrow's" newspaper business style, most writers give this comma death an approving nod. Some writers and some companies, however, still cling fiercely to their commas. Honor thy reader's wishes, if you know them.)

An acronym is an abbreviation of a multiword title by the initial letters of each word—e.g., NASA, IBM, ASAP, and so on. In general, an acronym (abbreviation by initial) should be written as all capital letters with no periods:

CEO
VP
Form the plural by adding a lower-case *s*:
All CEOs bestride this narrow world like so many colossi.
The VPs bestride pretty good, too.

Form the possessive of an acronym with an apostrophe and an *s*:

That's the CEO's Ferrari.
And that's the VP's Acura.

I.E. VERSUS E.G.

This is simple, but the two are often confused. And if you use one when you mean the other the knowledgeable reader will be distracted.

I.e. is usually read (translated) as "that is." (The two initials actually stand for "id est," Latin for "that is.")

E.g. is usually read (translated) as "for example." (The Latin is "exempli gratia.")

If you're confused about which to use, just substitute (in your mind or on the paper) the English phrase and see which phrase seems most appropriate for your circumstance. "That is" introduces a phrase that describes what you've just described, though from a bit different angle, i.e., an elaboration. "For example" introduces a series of examples of what you've just described, e.g., acronyms, abbreviations, etc.

The two letters are usually lowercased, with periods after each letter and no space between them, and set off with a comma before and a comma after. If the two-letter phrase begins your sentence, capitalize the first letter (only).

Its versus it's

This distinction is difficult to remember largely because there's no real logic here.

"Its" (no apostrophe) is possessive:

This is its home.

"It's" (with apostrophe) is the contraction meaning "it is":

It's a long way.

Most other possessives take an apostrophe:

This is Bob's house, where his son's dogs live.

"Its" does not take an apostrophe. Why? I don't know. But using either of the two incorrectly calls unwanted attention to your lapse.

Punctuation with Quote Marks

In the American style, which *is* what we use here in America, the comma or period goes inside the quotation mark:

This is "their finest hour."

Five

GETTING (AND KEEPING) THE READER'S INTEREST

We've discussed how too many business letters are boring. They're often wordy and far too often bloated with "safe" Business English.

Well, you can fix all that—liven up your letter with straightforward everyday language and active verbs—and still fail to make your business point with the reader. You must let the reader know *why* she should read your letter closely, and suggest to her *how* she should act after finishing it.

In this way, a business letter should mimic some of the traditional guidelines of effective advertising:

- Promise the reader a benefit, and
- Steer a specific response from him.

How often have you received a business letter, scanned it, and trashed it simply because you didn't see its pertinence to you right away? If someone asked you—right then, as your hand returned from its wastepaper toss to reach for the next letter in your in-box—you really couldn't tell the questioner just what the trashed letter proposed. The letter was vague, the day was busy. Result: trash.

Let's you and I peer over a businessperson's shoulder to see what kind of letters prick thoughts.

The *sine qua non* (i.e., the essential ingredient, literally "without which [there is] not") of an effective business letter is a clearly defined purpose. Don't be afraid to tell the reader right up front why you're writing. If you're unsure whether that purpose shows in your letter, you might want to simply state it:

I'd like to introduce to you our new line of underslung guided missiles and encourage you to try one before buying.

I'd like to bring you up to date with my activity on the Jones account for the last six months. Please share with me any suggestion you might have.

There are times, of course, when you might not want to explicitly announce your ultimate aim:

Through sheer persistence and continued annoyance, I hope to compel you to give me a try, if only to get rid of my dogged insistence.

This sort of up-front admission of long-term goals that conflict with the reader's desire rarely succeeds. Instead, announce your shorter-term aim:

I'd like to draw your attention to some strengths that other clients discovered only after purchasing our solar-powered swizzle stick. I hope this real-world feedback will move you to reconsider.

You need not always clearly announce your purpose in writing, especially if you're seeking to win someone over slowly and carefully. But, to make sure your letter is effective, *you* should know why you're writing. If you don't know, your reader certainly won't know (unless perhaps you're writing to your psychotherapist).

These aims should probably be laid out in the first paragraph of your letter, or as the first sentence of your second paragraph.

A busy reader—which includes just about every businessperson I know—will generally skim a letter first. If his interest is piqued he may read it again more closely. Unmoved, he will probably file the letter in the trash basket. That means you must pique his interest at the parts of a letter most often skimmed, and explain the bare bones of your persuasion there. A busy reader generally reads all of the first paragraph, the first few words of subsequent paragraphs, and some or all of the final paragraphs. Make your points in those places. Don't belabor the point.

Persuasive writing is driven to a large degree by genuine interest and enthusiasm. If you're not excited about what you're sharing in your letter, your reader certainly won't be. Seek some purpose that excites you: helping others try your fine product, making money, beating competitors, winning admiration. If you continually can find nothing that interests you in what you're writing about, seriously consider a different line of work.

Decide what *benefit* you are proposing to your reader. After all, your reader wants to know what's in it for *him*, not how *you* stand to gain. Helping your reader achieve this benefit, then, becomes the goal toward which you channel your enthusiasm. This is no cynical ploy. After all, commissions and self-interest aside, I believe most of us want to help our fellows—especially if helping *him* helps *us*.

The benefit should be couched to the reader in terms he relates to.

Acme's solar-powered swizzle stick can boost your employees' productivity 100 percent, eliminate the risk of carpal

*tunnel syndrome (and its profit-eating workman's comp claims),
and add customer-appeal theater to your watering hole. Saves
the ozone layer, too.*

or

*Maintain your ready access to capital by paying your bill
immediately. Our next year's models are ready to roll off the
line; settling past debts today will let you add these sure sellers
to your lineup tomorrow.*

Promising a businesslike benefit gives you another letter-
writing advantage. You need not resort to gimmicky attention-
getting devices, such as headlines:

Flash! World's greatest stapler now available!
or irrelevant sports analogies:
Clean valves: 7; Bacteria: 0.
or unbelievably global claims:
You'll never feed your dog again!

These gimmicks get attention, all right, but do they foster
the image your business wants? Probably not, unless you're in
the joy-buzzer business.

If you and the person to whom you're writing are friends,
you may want to use your first paragraph to reestablish a
chumminess. Note I said "reestablish." If you don't know
your recipient, don't attempt to chum up with him. Get to the
business "meat" of your letter. That's what he wants to know.
But if the two of you have worked together before, or if you've
talked on the phone and made a personal "connection," feel
free to use the first paragraph to catch up.

Dear Steve:
*I hear from Bernie you landed the Schmidlapp account.
Congratulations. Say "hello" to the Colonel for me when you
see him. You may remember he and I were fellow toilers at
Acme Industries back before the dinosaurs got their global
pink slips.*

or

Dear Mr. Ignatowski:
Good talking with you on the phone today. Congratulations
on your new position, and I'm sure you'll figure out how to
transfer calls soon—though it's a skill I'm rather shaky in, too.

Don't overdo the personal-rapport stuff. Sentiments such as
"I look forward to a productive relationship" glaze the
reader's eyes in a hurry.

Okay. First paragraph (or top of second): State your purpose. Tell 'em why you're writing.

Each paragraph after that, up to the final one: Build your
argument. How long should that building take? How long
should a letter be? It's hard to say. Obviously, if you're
proposing an untested phalanx of air-to-sea missiles to an
avowedly pacifist nation with a single-digit gross national
product, it's going to take a longer letter than would a note
urging an officer manager to restock with a few market-leader
staplers.

One hint on length, though: Shorter is better than longer.
When you have expressed your thoughts, stop. Don't pad.
Realize, however, that the line is tricky between repetition that
drives home your point and repetition that pads. For instance,
the two-word sentence above ("Don't pad.") is basically a
reiteration of the sentence right before it ("When you have
expresses your thoughts, stop."). But in this case, I feel the
short sentence works to *reinforce* the longer sentence before it.
Other critics might feel the second sentence is padding. I don't.
(Now *that* short sentence *is* a padding onto the longer sentence
before it.)

Short sentences are (generally) better than long sentences.
They make their point and stop, leaving the reader a break of
pace in which to internalize the idea. A short sentence keeps
the subject and the verb sufficiently close together that the
reader need not hunt back to see just what is being said.

But a constant barrage of "telegraphic" short sentences is
monotonous. Vary the lengths of your sentences. Remember,

your letter should reflect your personality: A page of curt sentences reads like a machine put the thoughts together; this is counterproductive. People prefer to work with people, not machines. Few readers will go "the extra step" for what seems to be a machine or in response to a machinelike letter.

Each of your sentences should contain just one chief thought. When you've articulated that thought, put a period after it and offer a second thought—in a second sentence. Repeat this process until you've built your thoughts into your argument. Your business letter aims to lead the reader through your thoughts; help him follow you one step at a time.

Help your reader distinguish your key points from your subsidiary ones. One way to do that is to mention the key points first—at the beginning of the letter and at the beginning of each paragraph. Such positioning also means that the reader who scans your letter will follow your thoughts.

Here's how that would look:

Date

Inside address

Dear Joe:

[First paragraph: Promise a benefit.]
Watering holes in your market have doubled their high-margin martini business with Acme's solar-powered swizzle stick. You can, too.

[Second paragraph: The key point in building your argument.]
(Lead idea:) This interest-stirring stick increases sales.
(Subsidiary ideas:) Its high-action, upscale image piques favorable patron attention. Spurs impulse purchases. Shifts patrons from lower-margin well drinks.

[Second paragraph: Second-most important point.]
(Lead idea:) The stick increases repeat business.
(Subsidiary ideas:) Patrons recall the stick. They remember where it was used. They come again.

[Third paragraph: Third-most important point.]
(Lead idea:) The stick boosts employee productivity 100 percent.
(Subsidiary ideas:) Stick quickly provides perfectly swizzled product. Easy cleanup. Convenient on-belt holster available.

[Fourth paragraph: Fourth-most important point.]
(Lead idea:) Stick eliminates carpal tunnel syndrome and its workman's comp claims.
(Subsidiary ideas:) Unique self-rotorization precludes repetitive-motion activity. Workman's comp is fourth-greatest cost to watering holes today. In one year, stick saved a 13-man hole $840,000 in reduced insurance costs.

[Fifth paragraph:] Fifth-most important point.
(Lead idea:) Saves the ozone layer, too.
(Subsidiary ideas:) Solar power produces no ozone-harming gases. Reduces calories expended by hole-men over swizzling by hand, reducing demand for calories otherwise replaced by slaughtered animal flesh or by water- and nutrient-demanding vegetables harvested probably by a fossil-fuel-burning tractor.

[Final paragraph: Sum and suggest action.]
(Lead idea:) The Solar Swizzler helps you make money. Let's talk at your hole on Monday afternoon.

(Subsidiary ideas:) I'll call you Friday to make an appointment. If not Monday, we'll schedule some other day. The stick is a proven profit-booster at holes just like yours.

Best wishes,

Bob Barr
Salesman

The final paragraph of your letter leaves the reader with a clear idea of what is expected of him. Who will contact whom? With what in mind? When? With how much expectation of further discussion on this issue and/or of making a decision then? Make it clear.

As we've said, the most important step toward keeping readers interested in what you're saying is to say something they're interested in. Say it plain, and with plenty of action.

Six

SALES LETTERS

It is often said that *all* business is *sales* business. After all, the entire premise of commerce is to take in money in return for some product or service. Research, marketing, production . . . all these business functions are but part of the product or service whose chief *raison d'être* is to be sold.

A sales letter, then, is probably the most important type of business letter your firm will produce. And, because the thread of sales permeates all business functions (some would say it permeates all human dealings), the sales letter format is applicable to most business functions, not just the direct selling function.

Sales letters are generally of two types: the personalized pitch and the mass mailing.

Mass mailings have boomed in recent years, tied directly to one thing: the boom in targeted mailing lists. Want to reach left-handed stamp collectors of Italian ancestry interested in fishing? Such a list can be compiled.

Mass-mailed letters vary from personal pitch letters in one important way: The mass mail letter must work harder to get and retain the reader's interest. And they must not alienate him with unbelievably hucksterish headlines and gimmicks. The blitz of "You've already won!" letters has tarnished the image of mass mailings.

The personal pitch letter generally can assume a certain amount of familiarity and rapport between letter writer and recipient. The writer can assume the reader will give him the benefit of the doubt in describing a subject of interest to them both.

Here, then, are the chief steps in building an effective sales letter.

1. Get the reader's attention.
2. Bring to reader's attention a need or desire of hers that is currently unmet. Describe how your product or service can meet that desire.
3. Convince her—through example or analysis—that your product will perform as promised.
4. Urge the reader to take specific action.

ATTRACTING ATTENTION

If you don't "hook" your reader in the first paragraph, you probably won't get a second chance at him. This means you must tap some desire or fear of the reader's. Does he want to make big money? Impress his peers? Keep his family safe? All these concerns—and more—offer you emotional buttons to push.

I suggest you treat your reader with respect and pitch your

implied benefit to him in a straightforward way. That means I advise against high-concept leads like shocker headlines or puzzling non sequiturs, such as:

Are your kids embarrassed by you? (Take our correspondence course and earn their respect with a prestigious new job.)
You may never need to work again! (Enter our sweepstakes.)

Instead, figure out what legitimate benefit your product offers—what desire it satisfies for its user. Position your product as a reasonable source of satisfaction to the reader. Remember to keep the reader's needs—not your own—driving your description. Don't just describe the features of your product. The reader is interested in *her* circumstances; she's not yet interested in looking at *your* offering.

Be professional, but be creative. Generally, your reader is under little compulsion to read your letter with enthusiasm—or even interest.

A recitation of facts and figures is rarely the best way to hook attention. Tell the reader a story; draw a verbal picture.

Let's look at some first-sentence hooks.

A question will generally pique readers' interest:

How're you fixed for blades, Mac?
or
Can your kids afford the college of their choice?
or
Did you ever wish you had more money . . . and more time to spend it?

Any businessperson is interested in what his competitor is doing:

Ajax Chemical boosted profitability 29 percent with the Little Fireplug valve toaster.

Human players keep reader interest more firmly fixed than do faceless corporate players:

Bob Strake, plant manager, then ordered three dozen more.

Conversation is often more dynamic than mere recitation of fact:

"They're small, but they're powerful," Strake says.

Detail helps:

"One every three feet of piping speeds product flow 14 percent."

Just don't forget to get permission from Ajax and Strake to quote their experience.

Thought-provoking wisdom from the past may stimulate fresh consideration in your reader:

Absence of occupation is not rest.
A mind quite vacant is a mind distress'd. —Cowper
. . . Try a college-study vacation at Oxford this year.

A "twist" ending to a surprising introductory idea is a crisp attention-getter:

Hate your job?
Maybe you need a new way of working—more organized, more well planned. Our computer software can help you do more, quicker.
or
Nobody loves you . . .
. . . As much as your family does. Who will take care of them if you were to go into the hospital? One of our many insurance plans will show your family you love them, too.

Just remember, your lead gains just the reader's *attention*. It cannot sell her on the value of your product. Follow through. And don't promise more than you can deliver.

DESCRIBE HIS NEED FOR YOUR PRODUCT

Surely there is something your reader needs, some itch he'd like scratched. If he's unaware of this small emotional vacuum, that's just because he hasn't yet met the right psychological salesman.

"Psychological" is often the key in tapping desire. People simply don't simply don't act solely (or wholly) from logic. You've got to tap some psychological need.

Let's read the mind of a busy businessperson who's just opened a letter that describes only the dry, logical virtues of our fictitious product, the Little Fireplug.

(*"A Little Fireplug valve warmer? Sure, probably makes sense. I'll look into it some day."*) [*When Tahiti freezes over. Fade to trash.*]

The facts-only letter simply didn't engage the busy reader's emotions. He didn't disagree or disbelieve the facts presented about the Little Fireplug, he just didn't get sufficiently stirred to break with his way of doing things.

What could we tell him about a valve warmer (not exactly a sex-charged product) to engage his emotions? Plenty.

We could play on his professional pride:

The leading firms in your industry use the Little Fireplug.

We could play on his professional fear:

Plant managers reluctant to keep up with new developments in valve maintenance are being fired, studies show.

We could play on his need to be loved or respected:

"The Little Fireplug tripled our productivity. It enabled us to keep this plant open and saving the community 1,500 jobs. And we owe it all to our far-sighted plant manager who specified Little Fireplug," exults a company president in your industry.

You get the idea: Describe to the reader an emotional benefit of your product or service.

Convince Her Through Logic

In person, those lucky few of us with compelling, magnetic personalities may be able to convince prospects of the verity of our cause through sheer repetition, a well-modulated voice, and hyperactive eyebrows. Obviously, through the paper medium, these strengths are useless.

Repetition, particularly, so often compelling in person (ask any mule), is simply exasperating on paper.

In the section above, on "hooking" the reader's desire, we emphasized the importance of tapping the prospect's emotions. Okay, she's interested, she *wants* it. Now we've gotta sell her a reason she should buy—a logical reason, one she can cite to justify his desire to herself and to her coworkers.

Unless your product is totally useless, this step of the sales letter should present little difficulty. "You know my methods, Watson, apply them," Sherlock Holmes used to say. "You know your product benefits, Mr. Salesman, list them."

Describe the features that make your product attractive. Back them up with numbers when possible.

. . . With over 35,000 square feet of cargo space—big enough to pack 1,500 traditional shipping crates.

. . . Producing 1,500 BTUs at an efficiency rating of 9.8 out of 10.

Back up the claims with reports from independent test labs or recognized experts.

. . . Ranked a "best buy" by Consumer Reports.

. . . Widely used by leading U.S. corporations, including Chemical Bank, General Motors, and IBM.

Or detail the particulars that stamp your product as a result of admirable design or thoughtful production:

. . . Built of 18-gauge stainless steel and TIG-welded in seamless beads guaranteed never to rust, dent, or twist.

Our firm has advised government agencies and corporations for over sixty years. Each of our consultants boasts at least ten years in your specific industry and has completed no fewer than one hundred hours of in-house training.

Guarantees and free samples make trial less a leap of faith.

Satisfaction guaranteed or your money back.
Try our product free for 30 days. Only then will we bill you.

Urge Action

The easiest thing for a reader to do upon finishing your letter is to throw it away. That's *not* what you want. You want him to act.

And you want him to act quickly: Your letter got him all fired up wanting your product; after he reads the next letter in his box he may forget you, or at least lose his enthusiastic edge.

Make it easy for your reader to respond. Suggest specific action he can take, and provide him a time frame in which to do it.

For more information, fill out the form below and drop it in the mail right now. A qualified sales representative will call with details of how you can immediately cut your undesired plastics by 30 percent. To learn more today, call 1-800-555-1234 and ask for Bob.

or

If you'd like to earn more money by working smarter, not harder, call 1-800-555-2468 now. I'll send you a cerebellar pep-up kit guaranteed to add 17 IQ points. Use it free for one full hockey season. If you don't agree the kit improves your life and your stickwork, return it and you owe us nothing. Act fast! We've only a few more left.

Note that these offers cost the sales prospect nothing. The letter is postage-paid; the phone call is a no-fee 1-800 number.

Just initial the post card below and we'll send you a Little Fireplug. Pay nothing now; we'll bill you later. See faster product flow soon; mail today.

Remember to avoid Business English in your sales letter. ("At this point in time I submit to you . . .") Let the sales letter show *your* personality. Be creative; be rigorous.

Seven

Letters
of Complaint

Things go wrong. Recently purchased items stop working. Or a shipped item is damaged when you receive it. Shipping clerks mail you the wrong item or bill you for a different item than you received. Or shippers refuse to acknowledge you've already paid your bill.

In this temporal life, a certain number of things are going to go wrong. It's unavoidable. And generally, it's unintentional.

In business, two trends have recently influenced the pace and number of errors. Computers now ease tracking a bewildering array of orders. Computer prompts help you quickly discover if an item is in stock to meet your need, and just where it's stored. This curbs errors. On the other hand, despite their speed and facility, computers are dumb. They make mistakes no human would. If a misentered stock number tells the computer to bill you one million dollars and 85 cents for a doorknob, you're likely to get just such a bill tucked into your doorknob shipper package. Computers curb a certain number of billing and stocking errors; computers spur a certain number of billing and stocking errors.

The second trend is the unavoidable but regrettable trend toward leanness and meanness in business staffing. For a variety of reasons, most businesses have cut back on the number of people doing jobs. Everyone, it seems, is running harder just to keep up. You know what happens when you rush: mistakes.

But as we said, whatever the current trends, mistakes always happen. When they do, realize probably no one is "out to get you." There's no cabal at XYZ Inc. plotting to send you one-eighth-inch widgets when you clearly specified one-fourth-inch widgets. If it happens once, write to request an exchange. If it happens twice, write to explain your disappointment. Perhaps at that time let XYZ understand your company can't afford such delays and if it happens again you'll be forced to order your widgets elsewhere. If XYZ can't meet your needs, perhaps you *should* move your trade elsewhere.

ANGER IS COUNTERPRODUCTIVE

A reputable company is prepared to make good on any reasonable error. All you need do is let the company know of your dissatisfaction and its causes. Suggest to the company representative what he can do now to make right the error. That's all. You need not "scream" at the company in your letter. Your anger is not something they can fix. No company rep can erase your anger, make it never to have happened. Concentrate instead on what can be done now, looking ahead.

Beware of making threats, especially in your initial letter.

Provide the company the opportunity to put right your situation first. If you have doubts that the company is wholly reputable, and it is subject to a regulatory oversight body—like the Better Business Bureau or a trade association—it is sometimes appropriate to mention you are willing to bring your case to such a body. But beware. Many of these threats are hollow: Most organizations have little or no control, other than censure, over unscrupulous businesspeople. And simple censure probably won't deter the truly unscrupulous businessperson.

No, probably the most effective threat you can make is not exactly a threat at all. Instead, it's a lure: the lure of your additional business.

An angry letter spiked with personal fury is not particularly effective. You're more likely to seem a dangerous lunatic than a responsible businessperson. Probably the least productive angry vow is the very one with which most such angry letters climax: "I'll never buy from you again!" By vowing this, you've just given the recipient a perfect excuse not to help you. What's he got to lose? You've already told him he's lost your business.

Here's how *not* to write a complaint letter:

> *Dear Moron:*
>
> *I've just received your shipment to me. The box was crushed! What do you do, meter-stamp it with an elephant's butt?*
>
> *Then when I opened the box, there was my order—NOT! I ordered left-handed widgets. You sent me right-handed ones. If I'd wanted right-handed widgets I would have ordered right-handed widgets, you idget.*
>
> *Are you guys drunk or stupid or what?*
>
> *I'm never going to order from you jerks again.*
>
> *Scathingly,*

What's the chief thing that's wrong with this complaint letter? Even more unproductive than its small-minded tone is that it offers no suggestion for making the mistake right. The letter writer does not mention if he's willing to ship the left-handed widgets back for exchange. He doesn't suggest the shipper phone him to clear up the misunderstanding. We don't even know if perhaps he's going to use the wrong-handed widgets and pay the bill, anyway! Probably the letter writer felt better after he got this venom out of his system. Probably the letter reader rolled his eyes and threw the letter away and forgot about it. Nothing got done.

Let's try it again, aiming at a businesslike result.

> *Dear Sir:*
>
> *This week I received from your company my order, which, according to the shipping invoice, is order number 070345, dated January 1.*
>
> *I had ordered 13 left-handed widgets. Your invoice specified left-handed widgets. Unfortunately, the box contained 13 right-handed widgets.*
>
> *I return to you the widgets I received, along with the invoice (of which I retain a photocopy). Please rush me 13 left-handed widgets in return.*
>
> *If there is any problem, please phone me immediately. My number is 1-800-555-1357.*
>
> *Sincerely,*

If the company's error has caused you hardship, let them know. But don't dwell on past injustice; focus instead on now making things right.

> *Dear Sir:*
>
> *On January 1 we ordered from you 25 silver maple trees for immediate delivery.*

On January 5, 25 trees were delivered by your agent Ace Trucking to the specified job site and my foreman accepted them. His men spent four working hours, planting four trees. On January 6 (today) I visited the site, where I saw that the 25 trees delivered were not silver maples, but were instead red oaks.

Red oaks are unacceptable.

Bob Jones, vice-president of Ace Trucking, suggests I must make any corrective arrangements with you, not him.

My work crew is no longer available. I must cancel my order for the 25 trees until other projects allow me to reschedule this tree planting.

Because of your error, I spent $100 for unproductive labor (5 men at $5 an hour for 4 hours). In partial recompense, I ask for a $100 discount on my next order of 25 trees.

Your red oaks are at the job site where delivered. I cannot guarantee their safety or their health, as most of them remained unplanted.

Please ask Ace Trucking to pick up the red oaks as soon as possible.

Please cancel my order—and my bill—for 25 silver maples.

Let me know right away if my $100 discount proposal is acceptable, and if so, please send me a letter verifying that. I hope to order again from you when my crew schedule allows.

Sincerely,

This letter is firm, but fair. The writer was obviously inconvenienced by another person's error, but he moves ahead with proposals for the future.

Eight

ADJUSTMENT LETTERS

In the previous chapter we looked at complaint letters—letters that describe errors or wrongs and ask for restitution. In this chapter we'll look at the letters that answer those complaint letters—adjustment letters.

Adjustment letters offer a company an excellent opportunity to foster goodwill among customers. After all, no customer particularly notices if the product he purchases performs as promised: That's expected. His attention is drawn more acutely to the company behind the product when something goes wrong. If the company handles his complaint well, it helps cement a customer relationship. Perhaps the customer will even pass along the word that the company treated him right.

If the company treats the complaint poorly—by ignoring it or rejecting it for unreasonable causes or simply replying rudely—you can be *sure* the customer will spread the word.

It's sometimes said that a satisfied customer will tell a friend. An unsatisfied customer will tell every friend he knows—and a certain number of strangers, too! And he won't be charitable.

Reply to any complaint promptly, with professional courtesy. Do not belittle any customer's complaint. Her dissatisfaction may seem foolish to you ("My flashlight failed after I used it in the shower"), but you must assume she is deeply distressed. On the other hand, if you plan to reject her demand, don't sympathize so feelingly that she is led to believe you plan to accept it.

In general, company policies toward adjustments fall into one of three categories:

1. Reasonable efforts are made to make reasonable amends to reasonable concerns.
2. The customer is always right. Keep him happy at all costs.
3. *Caveat emptor.* Let the buyer beware. No warranty is expressed or implied. You bought it; you keep it.

By far the most common business policy is the first one. It's also, obviously, the policy most fraught with ambiguity.

Once you decide whether or not you will meet the petitioner's request, describe how you reached that decision. What were the facts you considered? Length of ownership? Expected product lifetime? Expectation of quality for price charged?

SAYING NO

Be particularly scrupulous when you deny a request for adjustment. Explain how you decided her request was unreasonable. Offer an alternative settlement you feel is reasonable and describe how you arrived at that decision. Realize not everyone is "reasonable," and make efforts not to antagonize the petitioner in your denial.

Recognize the customer's emotional involvement in her appeal for adjustment. Recognize her humanness:

> *Dear Madam:*
> *Your request of January 1 that we replace your type-writer must be denied.*
> *Sincerely,*

A bit abrupt, eh?

Don't condescend to dismiss:

> *Dear Sir:*
> *We cannot meet your request that we replace your typewriter.*
> *You claim that the machine "never worked right" since you bought it. However, you present no evidence of that. You first mention its malfunction to us after you've owned it for two years. The warranty is good only for one year.*
> *Our policy does not allow us to make an exception in this case.*
> *Sincerely,*

The snide tone of this letter, with its references to "claim" and "evidence" impugn the integrity of the petitioner. No goodwill is won here. Also, the reader is left wondering in what cases policy *does* allow them to make an exception. Why not me, he wonders?

Avoid an adversarial tone in your denials. Surely there is something on which you and the petitioner can agree.

Quite often all petitioners genuinely want is to feel that someone recognizes their disappointment. They seek "validation," in the terms of popular psychology. Pop psyche books advise the sympathetic listener to nod and, basically, repeat what the petitioner says: "Yes, you feel bad." Perhaps your denial letter can at least offer the petitioner your recognition of her disappointment.

> *Dear Madam:*
>
> *I'm sorry to hear your MegaMax typewriter no longer works properly. After two years' use I'm sure its breakdown must disappoint you.*
>
> *However, the warranty on the MegaMax runs only for one year. Many MegaMaxes work for a great number of years; but by limiting your warranty coverage to only one year we are able to make the MegaMax available for a highly reasonable cost.*
>
> *We cannot extend your warranty coverage.*
>
> *May I suggest you investigate our GigaMax typewriter? It carries a lifetime warranty. Or perhaps you might ask your dealer about an extended warranty on a new MegaMax, for a low additional cost.*
>
> *Best wishes,*

Obviously, you must walk the line between sympathy and foolishness. Inappropriately heartfelt sympathy may strike the reader as pandering condescension.

As with any business letter, suggest to the reader some followup course of action (". . . investigate our GigaMax"). This keeps the reader's attention focused ahead, rather than on past "injustices." And a suggestion makes the writer seem concerned for the reader's welfare, when otherwise the writer might seem caught simply in stout denial.

Handled well—a reasonable rationale for refusal offered in a courteous tone—an adjustment denial letter need not damage a business relationship.

SAYING YES

A letter that grants an adjustment is much easier to write. After all, you're telling the reader good news—of a sort. It's not, of course, wholly unalloyed good news—the consumer's best news would have been performance as expected and no need to write a complaint letter at all. Remember, then, that a "yes" letter has an aim other than just saying yes. It aims to foster continued goodwill.

First, though, let the reader know you are granting his requested adjustment. If you're granting his request in full, let him know immediately:

Dear Mr. Disgruntled:

Thank you for letting us know of your difficulties with the Ajax Mighty Mite. We're happy to send you a new one, which will be mailed out today.

Ajax strives to offer a top-quality product. Occasionally, however, unforeseen problems impair even the best-designed and -manufactured products. That's why Ajax offers the most complete warranty in the industry.

I apologize for your inconvenience. I'm sure the replacement Mighty Mite will give you years of satisfaction.

If you have any suggestions of how we might improve our product or its service, please don't hesitate to write me personally.

We seek to be the best in the business.
Sincerely,

If you are offering the reader a partial grant of his request—which means, of course, a partial denial—you may want to establish your logic before you describe your action:

Dear Mr. Disgruntled:

Thank you for letting us know of your difficulties with the Ajax Mighty Mite. We design Mighty Mite to give years of trouble-free flashlight service.

As you probably know, the Mighty Mite is designed to work with a 20-watt bulb. It is supplied with this type bulb and details inside the screw cap specify a 20-watt replacement bulb. The package label on replacement bulbs of all leading manufacturers describe the flashlight models appropriate for each bulb.

A 40-watt kryptonite bulb will burn the contacts of any flashlight designed for a 20-watt bulb. This is what happened with your Mighty Mite.

I'm sorry, but we cannot grant your request for a replacement Mighty Mite. Our warranty cannot extend to unforeseen modifications of its working parts.

To get your Mighty Mite back on its feet, however, I'm happy to send you new battery contacts (enclosed). Simply screw the old contacts out and screw the new ones in with new fasteners. All instructions are attached.

This should give your Mighty Mite a new lease on many years of "brilliant" life.

Sincerely,

Notice that the letter writer above did not disparage the claimant: He didn't call him a lunkhead for using what its package clearly called inappropriate bulbs. He didn't mincingly quote warranty chapter and verse to the claimant. Instead, he described the logic behind his decision.

Notice, too, the letter writer made it quite clear that he was rejecting the claimant's request (for replacement), and he made it clear what he was offering instead (new contacts only).

Nine

COLLECTION LETTERS

A collection letter seeks payment—generally overdue payment.

The tone of a collection letter varies, depending chiefly on how long the payment has been overdue and on the businessperson's estimate of whether the debtor has overlooked payment or is seeking to escape his responsibilities.

Rather than a single model of collection letter, each company probably produces a series of collection letters—to be mailed in sequence as the debt remains unpaid. The series does not necessarily get more strident, or more threatening, as it progresses. Instead, each letter in the series may simply seek to push different emotional buttons.

You probably don't want to threaten or alienate your

debtors. Most people want to pay their debts. They know it'll make their life easier in the long run. Probably, too, they want to continue doing business with you, as soon as they get their debts cleared up. You want this, too. Assume the attitude that the two of you are working together to clear up past debts and understandings so that life—and business—can go on.

INITIAL REMINDERS

The first collection note sent out almost always assumes the debtor has simply overlooked his bill:

> *Dear Sir:*
>
> *Have you overlooked your recent bill? For your convenience, I attach another copy.*
>
> *If your check has already been mailed, accept our thanks.*
>
> *Sincerely,*

If your company's policy is to stop credit until such debts are paid, let the debtor know that and that you will consider him a welcome customer after payment.

> *Dear Sir:*
>
> *Have you overlooked your recent bill? For your convenience, I attach another copy.*
>
> *We value your business. Please help us balance our books so we can continue to serve you.*
>
> *As soon as we receive your check, your charge account will be automatically reactivated. Until then, we must suspend your account.*
>
> *Sincerely,*

or

Dear Madam:

Please consider this a friendly reminder that there is an outstanding balance of $100 for services rendered by Ajax Pest Control on 1/1/93.

Please send your payment in the attached envelope, or call our office to discuss other arrangements.

Sincerely,

MORE-POINTED COLLECTION LETTERS

You've reminded the debtor of his debts and you've asked him to discuss his difficulties or confusion: Still nothing. It's time to push some emotional buttons.

A number of emotions may move a debtor to cough up. Perhaps a simple appeal to his pride:

Dear Sir:

The ABC Store has long prided itself on its appeal to some of the region's most discriminating customers—like you. You and your peers enable ABC Store to offer the finest merchandise and the most accommodating service in the Tri-County area.

Please help us continue to count you among this elite. Bring your account up to date so we can continue to serve you.

A postage-paid envelope is enclosed. Please send us a check today. And come see us again soon.

Sincerely,

He may respond to a commonsense threat to his credit rating:

Dear Sir:

As a responsible person in the community you realize the

importance of a sound credit rating. With it, access and the freedom to choose is yours. Without it, you risk being locked out of your dreams.

Don't jeopardize your credit rating. Our books show an overdue balance of $100 against your name.

Pay soon so you can enjoy the benefits of recognized responsibility.

Sincerely,

Or perhaps you can lure her into settling up with the promise of anticipated store benefits:

Dear Madam:

Famous designer suits 50 percent off! Handbags and leather goods at one-third savings!

Sound good? Well, it's coming up at ABC Store's summer clearance sale, July 4 through 14.

We want you to share in these bargains. But before we can extend you the freedom of credit, we must clear up your outstanding balance of $100.

Do you hunger for the sleek feel of vinyl-and-spandex bicycle shorts? We've got some beauts going out the door at reductions of up to 75 percent. Pay your bill today, and impress your friends with your fashion savvy.

Sincerely,

Sometimes bills are delayed because the debtor simply can't pay then, despite his eagerness to do so. Perhaps the two of you can reach a flexible arrangement.

Dear Sir:

Your account is $100 overdue.

Is there confusion over the bill? Its date? Its amount?

Please call me to discuss this lapse before it grows burdensome—to you and to us. Perhaps we can work out a schedule of payments. Let's work together.

Sincerely,

ULTIMATUMS

By the time final-gasp ultimatums are being mailed, probably other collection methods are being employed, too: phone calls, personal interviews, telegrams, and the like. These media carry a bit more attention-demanding clout that the mail. Also, personal confrontation—by phone or in person—forces the debtor to make *some* sort of response toward resolving the impasse. A letter, as readers of this book know well, is often readily ignored.

Ultimatum letters are frequently mailed special delivery or by registered mail—both to confirm their receipt and to convey to the debtor its importance. Often the letters are signed by a top executive of the firm that's trying to collect.

Ultimatum letters describe just that—an ultimatum, or threat. The threat may be: report to a collection agency or an attorney, repossession or garnishee of debtor's salary (where legal). Generally a precise deadline for avoiding the ultimatum is described—often a week or ten days.

Make sure the debtor understands he still has the power to avoid the ultimatum—by paying his debt. Describe your reluctance to impose the ultimatum; it is easier for both of you if he were to pay up first. Be careful not to make a threat you cannot enforce: Give the debtor a genuine reason for paying up.

Dear Mr. Detter:
We have received no correspondence from you regarding your $100 debt with our company.

Unless we receive full payment by June 15, we must report your delinquency to our collection attorneys, who will pursue legal suit, which may include an attachment of your salary.

We prefer not to take this extreme step. You are empowered to prevent it. Please remit payment in full to this office by June 15.

Only full payment by that date will stop this process.

Sincerely,

or

Dear Mr. Detter:

Unless we receive your payment of $100 within 10 days we will be forced to turn the collection of your account over to Ajax Collections. Generally, any business recorded with Ajax is precluded from credit business with any other firm in the state.

This would, no doubt, cripple your business.

If we receive your check within 10 days, we will not turn over your files to them. If we do not receive your payment, you can expect to hear from Ajax's legal team soon thereafter.

It's your move.

Sincerely,

The series of collection letters has now run its course. The first letters were friendly—even humorous, perhaps. The insistence on the importance of payment increased with each letter. The final letter threatened specific, undesirable action.

But each letter asked the reader to pay his bill.

Ten

REQUEST FOR INFORMATION

Letters that seek information are probably second only to sales letters for the title of most-frequent business letters.

From the recipient's point of view, information letters fall into one of two categories:

- Rote-response letters. The inquirer seeks information that the recipient already has in mailable form—a brochure, a booklet, or a form letter, for instance.
- Special-request letters. These seek "one-off" information that must be answered in a personalized letter. Here the inquirer is asking for a special helping of the businessperson's two most valuable commodities: his thoughts and his time.

The inquirer cannot always know into which category his letter will fall. But he should always aim to make his request as specific as possible, and as simple to answer as possible.

ROTE-RESPONSE INQUIRIES

Probably the easiest inquiry letter to write—because you know it's the easier letter to answer—is an inquiry solicited by your target. Perhaps the company ran an ad asking readers, "For more information, ask for booklet X-100," or something. That's easy:

> *Dear Sir:*
> *Please send me your free booklet X-100, "How to Tie Better Shoelaces," as described in your ad on page 14 of the July issue of* Footwear News.
> *Sincerely,*
> *Bob Seeque*
> *123 Main Street*
> *Hometown, NE 50505*

Note that Bob described where he saw the solicitation (July's *Footwear News*) and the full title of the brochure. Surprisingly often, firms that solicit your requests are ill equipped to process them. If your letter gets routed to someone who does not recognize the reference to X-100, this information helps him help you.

Note, too, that Bob included his mailing address on his letter. If your letter is sent on letterhead, this may not be necessary. But do not assume the firm will get your address from your return address on the envelope: It was probably thrown away.

If you seek information that is not specifically touted in an ad or elsewhere, try even harder to describe your needs *specifically*.

> *Dear Sir:*
>
> *I seek information on your lineup of 386-chip computers.*
>
> *Would you please send me details of your 386 models, particularly those appropriate for personal use, including performance details and a list of add-on options.*
>
> *Please include a list of suggested prices, and/or the name and phone number of a dealer in my area who can quote prices for me.*
>
> *I plan on buying a computer soon. I hope one of your models fits my needs.*
>
> *Sincerely,*

This writer does not know just what form of information he can expect: brochures, flyers, trade journal reprints, or perhaps a personal-response letter. He tries to describe his search as explicitly as possible. Because he understands the reader exercises some discretion in just how hard he works to satisfy the request—whether he slips in to the return envelope just one general-interest brochure or he hunts down four highly specific ones, for instance—the writer subtly urges the reader to make an extra effort by promising him a potential benefit, however tenuous: in this case, a sale.

SPECIAL-REQUEST INQUIRIES

A special-request inquiry is, basically, one that requires time and creativity to answer. The example above of the computer-info letter might well be a special-interest inquiry. The writer has little way of knowing if the reader has an information pack that perfectly suits his request—the reader need simply write the addressee's name to process it—or if the reader must rifle through files, photocopy some, and compose a letter to meet the request.

There are many requests any reasonable person would know will require special action. They obviously cannot be answered by brochures or flyers. Here, then, the writer should make special efforts to ease the response.

You generally cannot expect a businessperson to spend hours answering your unsolicited questions. Ask the most specific questions possible, to prompt short, pointed responses. If appropriate, enable the reader to check off her answers: yes, no, scale of 1 to 5, and the like.

How many gallons of nonalcoholic beer does your company sell in a year? (gallons)

What percentage of your total beer sales is that? (percent)

Do you know if more men or women buy your nonalcoholic beer: [   ] men   [   ] women

Do you know the percentage of men and women drinkers of your nonalcoholic beer: % men   % women

On a scale of 1 to 5, where 1 is least important and 5 is highly important, how important is your advertising in driving sales of your non-alcoholic beer: 1 2 3 4 5

How important is taste: 1 2 3 4 5

How important is price: 1 2 3 4 5

Finally, would you comment on your company's overall marketing tack to nonalcoholic beer—all comments are welcome:

Help your reader ''see'' you when you ask her to do you the favor of answering your questions. Describe why you're asking.

I am a graduate student in marketing at Brew University and I am doing my master's thesis on the marketing of nonalcoholic beer. I'd like to tap the expertise of you and your counterparts at the other top three brewers.

Describe a potential benefit to the reader of taking the time to help you.

I'll take the liberty of sending you a copy of my thesis, on the chance you find it interesting.
or
I understand you, too, earned your marketing degree at Brew U. You'll be happy to know the dining hall still serves BrewskiCo products after 6:00 P.M.
Please help a new generation of beer marketers with your insights.

Finally:

A self-addressed, stamped envelope is enclosed.
Your help is greatly appreciated. Go Brew!

Eleven

JOB-SEARCH LETTERS

The time to start writing businesslike letters is *before* you get a job. The practice starts with a businesslike job-search letter.

We call them *job*-search letters, but really they're *interview*-search letters. And, let's hope, interview-*thanks* letters. Almost no one gets a job from his first letter. Almost no one gets a job without an interview.

The interview-search letter is generally called a *cover* letter because it is sent attached atop your résumé. It's almost always a single page—no more.

We won't discuss here how to write your résumé, which is covered in another No Nonsense Guide, *How To Write A Résumé*. We'll simply note that a cover letter generally amplifies some aspect of your résumé that is of especial interest to the particular potential employer—your education or your job experience that would seem to offer the employer the greatest insight into your benefit *to him*.

The cover letter and résumé are together a sales letter. You are selling your abilities. You are selling the potential value of an interview with you.

NETWORKING LETTERS

Before we look in depth at cover letters and interview thank-you letters, let's take a look at a form of letter-linked job search that has grown more common in the last ten years or so: networking.

Networking simply means letting as many appropriate people as possible meet you and know you seek a job. Usually you start with people you know, and from them you get names of *their* friends and coworkers who might be in a position to know of job opportunities for which you'd be appropriate. You seek to meet with these people, to discuss business with them, acquaint them with your abilities, and get from them more names to contact. You are not expressly looking for a specific job when you network.

So you're not asking for an interview. Instead, you are *imposing* on someone to ask her opinions on her field. Why would anyone consent to be imposed on? Two reasons: as a favor to you or the person who suggested her name, and to enjoy sharing her thoughts with a respectful, interested audience—you.

Dear Ms. Field:

Dick Coworker suggested you might be gracious enough to share with me some of your thoughts and experiences of the latex clothing business. After 8 years in the vinyl undergarment industry, I'm investigating opportunities in related fields. Before I can do that, though, I'm trying to get some background on the field from thoughtful observers like you. I'd certainly appreciate hearing your thoughts about how the industry is configured and who the major players are.

I'll take the liberty of calling later this week to ask if you can find a few minutes to talk with me in your office.

Sincerely,

Do *not* attach your résumé to your networking letter. Make it clear you are *not* asking for a job interview. Instead, you want to—as you said—talk with her about the industry in general and perhaps about her company in particular. It is an informational interview. Your objective is to acquaint yourself with people who might hear of jobs.

NOT I, BUT THEE

The cover letter with résumé is *not* a networking tool; its aim to get a *job* interview, not an *informational* interview.

As with any sales letters, keep the emphasis of your cover letter on promising a benefit *to the reader*. You are trying to convince the employer you can meet his needs; he doesn't necessarily have the time to work with you simply because *his* firm meets *your* needs—nor it is his responsibility to succor you in this way. Tough, but true.

It's difficult to keep your eye on your potential employer's needs in your search letter. Probably all you can think is, "I want that job," not "The XYZ Company would certainly benefit from my talents." Well, a bit of "hunger" is admired in a job seeker, but remember, you're selling, not buying. Would you buy from a salesman whose pitch centered on, "I really want you to buy this. I need the job satisfaction and the money?" Probably not.

Keep the emphasis on the benefit you would bring the company.

Getting Started

Let the reader know right away why you are writing: You are interested in a job and in a job interview. Don't be coy in describing your aim and don't pretend you seek just an informational interview. There need be no embarrassment in seeking a job interview.

It's often hard to know just how to begin your cover letter. You probably feel a lot of pressure to strike just the right tone—an impossible task since there is no single appropriate tone.

How critical is a cover letter? It depends. Some potential employers value them highly in gauging an applicant's appeal. Others barely glance at them and focus only on the résumé. But if your résumé isn't your strength in positioning you for the job, lead with a good strong cover letter.

Probably the most common introduction is a description of what about you most suits you for the job you seek. This may be your experience or your education, or perhaps simply your personal character.

> *Dear Sir:*
>
> *My three years' experience as assistant manager of Bob's Little Store has given me an understanding of the midget clothing retail business I feel would prove to be of real value to you at Tina's Teeny Toggery.*

Or you might drop the name of a mutual acquaintance right at the beginning (as we did in our networking letter).

> *Dear Madam:*
>
> *Jim Donnybrook in your marketing department tells me a junior marketing position is likely to open there soon. My*

recent marketing degree from Kickapoo State might war-
rant your attention.

Or you might simply ask if the reader would value your
abilities.

> *Dear Sir:*
>
> *Would you value a knowledgeable, motivated salesman?*
> *My years of success in selling widgets enables me to*
> *develop new customers for a leading widget-accessory firm.*

Your résumé will detail your *experience*. So perhaps you
should open your cover letter with an outright expression of
your *attitude*.

> *Dear Sir:*
>
> *I'm very excited about the assistant marketer's position*
> *you described in the* Times. *My four years' internship at the*
> *National Cheesecutters Institute has provided me a detailed*
> *familiarity with cheese-slicer marketing.*

BODY OF LETTER

After you've established in your reader's mind why you're
writing, spend a paragraph or two elaborating on the strengths
that suit you for the job. This information is basically a bit of
expanding on the two or three elements described telegraphi-
cally on your résumé that give you greatest ability *for this
particular job*.

For instance, your résumé may list that your next-to-last job
was as a salesman at Bob's Appliance Shoppe, described there
simply as "Sold household appliances of all types. Top
salesman eight months out of twelve." If you were applying for
a job with Hotshoe Ironing Board Company, you might describe:

At Bob's Appliance, I was responsible for the iron department, where I grew fully familiar with the attributes of all models of all leading manufacturers. In helping customers choose an iron, I grew highly knowledgeable about what people want in the ironing experience.

Here in the body of your cover letter is your opportunity to show you understand the reader's business—both of the industry in general and his company in particular. Don't try to show off by simply telling the reader something he already knows. ("Your firm, Acme Radiator, is a $14-million company.") Instead, use your familiarity to make a point of your own. ("My strength in juggling a number of tasks would probably be of particular value at an industry-leading $14-million company like Acme Radiator.")

The body of the letter is also the place to show a bit of your personality. If you're sober and meticulous, write in a terse style with few, well-chosen words. If you're chatty and excitable, write in a fittingly "talky" style. If you show a little personality and liveliness in your letter, you're almost sure to stand out among the pile of dull, formulaic cover letters the interviewer has likely already received. Be lively-minded and excited. But don't risk seeming flip or cynical.

THE CLOSE

As with a classic sales letter, in the closing paragraph of your cover letter you ask for the sale. In this case, you're asking for an interview. You've made your case already; now is the time to ask for results.

Be explicit in what you're asking. Don't be coy.

May I meet with you to discuss my potential value to your company? I'll call you later this week to seek to set a time. Please feel free to call me before then.

THANK-YOU LETTER

Congratulations. You got an interview. Now it's time to write another letter. This one's simple. It should be short. Thank the interviewer for her valuable time and attention. To refresh her memory of which fresh-faced eager applicant you were, you might allude to one thought the two of you discussed—it need not have been work-related. Repeat your eagerness to do a good job and let her know you hope to hear from her soon.

Good luck.

Twelve

THE
BUSINESS MEMO

So far, we've talked chiefly about business *letters*. Most of the points we discussed apply directly to memos, too: Both letters and memos benefit from using lively, readily understood sentences to build a pointed argument aimed at a clearly defined purpose.

Obviously, some of the points we investigated do *not* apply to memos. The business block page layout, certainly, is not called on in memo writing. And job-search correspondence, for instance, is rarely done through memos.

How do memos differ from letters?

- They are laid out on the page differently. This may seem like an inconsequential difference, but often this format difference is the only real distinction between two series of paragraphs that express similar sentiments.

- Memos are generally distributed only within your company. If you're writing to someone outside your company, put your thoughts into letter form; if to someone "on your team," work them up as a memo.
- Memos generally assume a greater familiarity between sender and recipient. We've discussed how the "tone" of your business letters should reflect the comparative status between the sender and recipient: A junior executive writing a president of an outside firm would assume a more "formal" tone that he would in addressing another junior executive, or than would a letter passed between two company presidents. Since within any one company the two of you share the same goals (at least on the surface), your memo can assume a bit more comradely tone. Probably, too, you know well the in-house fellow you're writing to. Your writing reflects this familiarity.
- Memos are generally *slightly* more brisk in their phrasing than are comparable letters. The difference is but slight because, by following the suggestion of this book, you've already rid your business writing of formalities and pomposity.

Memos are generally designed as a "quick read." But don't let that impulse pull you into writing a telegram. Short, staccato bursts of sentences may look brisk and efficient, but too often bare-bone phrasing leads instead to reader confusion. Time spent puzzling out obscure bits can quickly outpace the time saved in dropping a seemingly expendable word. Also, confusedly telegraphic thoughts are easily misunderstood. Remember the movie idol's joking response to the misrouted telegram "How old Cary Grant?" I'm sure the questioner wished he'd spent the extra nickel for the verb when he got by return telegraph, "Old Cary Grant just fine. How you?"

- Finally, memos are directly political. They are shared

among your peers and higher-ups, the people who gauge your suitability for additional responsibility—and promotion. A business letter may fail to bring in a sale or to close a deal, but that failure is still yours to later explain or justify in-house. Rarely will an outside prospect route your business letter back to your boss with a penned note, "Look at the lame effort your employee made to do business with me." A business letter is the face you show your clients and customers. A business memo is the face you show your boss and coworkers.

In-house memos, then, require *at least* the same care as outgoing letters. Clear, purposeful memos can make careers.

The number and range of those clear, purposeful memos that any one businessperson must write in the course of a day or a week varies. Some people write twenty a day; other workers may write no more than one a month. One determinant of the number of memos you write is simply your company's culture. Some companies—or bosses—prefer that any sentiment more far-reaching than "Nice tie, Bob," is put into memo form. Other firms—especially smaller ones—prefer memos passed only on items that quote numbers (prices, closing dates, sales totals) or similar pledges (so the memo can be pulled out and waved at you when you miss your target).

Memos have suffered a bad rap in the corporate-efficiency press for many years. They're too often time-wasting, the stopwatch-clicking engineers tell us. The use of memos should be curbed, we're advised (most often in a memo from the big boss). Instead, we're urged to pick up the phone or walk down the hall. "Do It Now," urged the hand-stitched sampler on the office wall of every nineteenth-century tycoon-wannabee.

Which is mightier in-house: tongue or pen?

- Conversation is generally much quicker than writing a memo.
- Conversation allows you to react immediately to your audience.

- Your listener can't later insist he never got your conversation.

But:

- A memo provides a paper trail (for good or ill).
- A memo can readily reach more people with the same effort (through the powerful "cc:" line).
- A memo—any writing, really—forces you to think more clearly about both your understanding and your goal.

This last point should be the greatest drive behind your decision to write a memo rather than pick up the phone. A memo powerfully summarizes: "Here's what we've done; here's our crossroads; here are our options. What do you say?"

Yet often the greatest drive to write a memo rather than talk it out is to make sure you get credit for the idea. A memo with your name on it links you strongly to its contents, even if they're not truly original to you. The "head office" generally credits the memo writer with the idea, not the guy who first floated it in the cafeteria.

Nobody really likes memos. No one particularly likes to write them and certainly no one likes to read them. Business letters, we said in an earlier chapter, have one chief problem: They're boring. Business memos' chief problem is related: They're too long.

They're too long often because they're *too* political. You're writing to tell your boss what *he* needs to know; it's easy to try to tell him *everything you* know. Some companies try to curb politics-stuffed memos by issuing "action briefings." If it helps you to sleek your memos, think of them by that name.

How long should a memo be? A few years ago, a large American corporation issued an edict: No memo can exceed one page. What happened? Well, the few 8-point (tiny) typewriter balls that had been sitting overlooked in secretaries' desks were found. Margins were whittled to slivers. And a great flood of memos were suddenly headed, "Additional information on . . ." These efforts sidestepped the spirit of the one-page-memo memo, but the idea is sound.

The standard way to organize a memo is:

1. Tell the reader why you are writing. ("The low sales figures for buttons in December [attached] require us to seriously rethink our business.")

2. Explain—in only the level of detail in which your reader is interested—how your thinking was spurred and where it has led. ("Ajax, Inc., our biggest client, has shifted its market emphasis from ladies' shirtwaists to men's spats.")

3. Summarize quickly, and announce your conclusions or your suggestions for action. ("Our own research confirms that of Ajax: Shirtwaists are dead. Mr. Ajax has indicated he is interested in our line of spat-spec buttons. Please give me details of our spat-spec button inventory and additional sources of appropriate manufacturers, including current prices.")

Basically, then, a memo should sum up a situation, describe the options, and request a specific response.

As with a business letter, make sure your reader understands what is expected of him. Describe as specifically as possible what you are asking him to do: research competitors' price points, broaden his customer base, work harder, retabulate his figures, etc. If appropriate, set a timetable for completion: by next Wednesday, before next quarter, let's meet to discuss—Is next Thursday at 10:00 okay?—Let me know today, please.

LAYOUT

Most companies provide paper or forms specifically for memos. If your company issues memo paper, and if most employees use it, you use it, too. Even if you think the form is ugly or awkward, use it if that ugly, awkward form is how the people in your office announce among themselves that the piece of paper that just landed in your in-box is a memo.

One reason I stress the value of using "official" memo forms is that computers enable the writer to spec out his own memo form, with an attractive variety of typesizes and styles. The problem then is that memos from no two sources look alike. A reader's attention is distracted by the unexpected format, subtly undercutting the memo's purpose as a quick read.

The "header" of a memo form generally asks the writer to announce four things:

Date:
To:
From:
Subject: (or Re:)

We've discussed how a memo is a bit less formal a document than a business letter. Here's the first place we have to balance that casualness with professionalism.

DATE

I suggest you write the month—fully or in abbreviation—and I suggest you provide the year. Memos sometimes are resurrected surprisingly long after they were written: A notation of the year can ease a great deal of potential confusion. I advise against using digit-only date (e.g., 1/12/93) for three reasons: 1) It's too easy to get confused. It's easier to slip into a typo—label a letter for month 5 when you mean month 6—than it is to unthinkingly type, say, May when you mean June. 2) Not everyone instinctually knows the numbers of the month. If in December you were looking at memo dated 4/12, would you have to count out on your fingers to confirm it was written in April? 3) Does your company have an overseas office? If so, you know that outside the U.S. writers place the day *before* the month. A memo from Des Moines dated

4/12/83 was typed on April 12th. One from Düsseldorf dated 4/12/83 (more likely, 4.12.93) was typed December 4th. Do you need this headache?

TO/FROM

How casual: To: Bob? To: Bob Davidson? To: Bob Davidson, Director of Marketing? In an office of great size, or in a memo of potential pass-along importance, include the sender's (and your) last name. Similarly, in highly fileable memos or in memos likely to be photocopied and passed along through the recipient's department, you might want to include titles.

Your memo may be directed to more than one person. You may list the names there, either in a regular horizontal line set off by commas or in a vertical series. With a highlighter or a pen, mark off a name in sequence on each copy, to ease distribution.

List the names alphabetically or in descending order of corporate hierarchy—or a mix of the two systems if one or two of the route names are obviously eminent, followed by alphabetical names of muddled hierarchical order.

If its target audience is a group of people defined by their group, address the memo that way, not through an exhaustive list of names.

   TO: All employees
or
   TO: Regional sales staff

If for ease of distribution each memo should be marked with an individual's name, pen in a name at the top of each memo somewhere, or list the names of the target recipients under a ''cc'' at the end of the memo and highlight or tick them off. (See more about cc's later in this chapter.)

SUBJECT LINE

Write the subject line last: that's what readers read first. And by writing your subject line after you've fully thought through your memo by writing it, you'll have a better idea of precisely what your subject is. (Points sometimes shift in the process of being articulated.) Describe in your subject line your point, not just your topic area.

Re: Coconut shipment is lost
not
Re: Coconut shipment

You might even consider a bit of a "tease" in your subject line.

Re: Can we find our coconuts?

BULLETS AND LISTS

Since memos are a bit less formal than letters, and since they aim for the quick read, a bulleted or numbered list of points is a highly effective way to present information.

We hold these truths to be self-evident:
* *All men are created equal.*
* *They are endowed by their creator with certain inalienable rights, among which are:*
    –life,
    –liberty, and
    –the pursuit of happiness.
* *To secure these rights, governments are instituted among men, deriving their just powers from the consent of the governed.*

- *Whenever any form of government becomes destructive of these ends, it is the right of the people to alter or abolish it.*

Or, with numbers:

Each "Welcome to New York" packet contains:
1. *An "I heart NY" button*
2. *A Port Authority bus terminal floor plan*
3. *A bus schedule*
4. *A calendar of events*
Enjoy.

You may begin each bulleted point with an uppercase letter or, if the bulleted item is not a complete sentence, with a lowercase letter. You may end each bulleted point with a period, a comma, a semi-colon, or no punctuation at all. Choose the style you feel is easiest to read.

Subject headlines or subheads help the reader grasp the scope of your memo before he actually reads it, and these visual cues help him zero in on subjects that interest him. These sorts of reader aids are of questionable professionalism in a business letter, but are wholly acceptable—nay, desirable—in a memo.

How Much Background?

Because a memo is passed among coworkers, the writer and the reader share a certain level of common understanding behind the subject being discussed. The writer must decide how much of this background to recapitulate in his memo. Too much background and the reader grows impatient; too little and he's left confused.

As with a business letter, keep your eye on your point. Alas, this rigor of point pursuit may be more difficult to impose on a memo than on a business letter. A letter generally seeks a response of its reader: meet me, send me, buy from me. In contrast, the aim of many memos is strictly informational: Here's our vacation policy; this is the status of the Jones account; here are my recommendations for our restructuring. This "backgrounding" function of a memo tempts the writer to just . . . begin at the beginning and tell you all he knows that relates even remotely to the subject.

Instead, discipline your memos. Summarize your major point in your lead:

Date: January 1, 1993

To: Joe
    Jim
    Jerry

From: Bob

Re: Restructuring for greater customer service

With Hank leaving us, now is a good time to reconsider how we handle some things, including our customer complaints. I suggest that, rather than appointing a single employee to answer all customer complaints (our current practice), we make each salesperson responsible for his particular customers' complaints.

This new system should be more efficient and should help our customers feel they get more sensitive after-sale service. The customer will work with only one company representative—one he already knows and trusts.

Our old system—built around a central customer-complaint office (i.e., Hank)—worked well in making sure the right forms were filled out in-house and filed with the right departments. However, Hank could not be—and was not—

familiar with the initial sale, nor was he intimate with the customers' business and how our equipment was configured to fit it. Miscommunication between the customer and Hank naturally sometimes resulted. This frustrated customers.

In this highly competitive market we cannot afford to frustrate a customer, particularly one already disappointed in our product performance.

I realize this shift in responsibility will place an additional burden on our salespeople. Perhaps we can investigate simplifying our current forms and filing practices to ease the burden somewhat.

But in the long run, this shift should help the salespeople boost customer satisfaction—and repeat sales. And it's a lot easier to keep a customer than to replace a customer.

Let's meet to discuss this proposed change. How about Friday at 3:00? Please call me immediately to confirm or reschedule.

> *cc: Ben Barnes [writer's boss]*
> *Hank Herlihy [departing coworker]*
>
> *bcc: Stan Kaplan [firm's attorney]*

Notice how Bob quickly reviewed the background of this issue ("With Hank gone," and "Our old system . . .") without detailing unnecessary background. Bob described the chief facts and ideas on which he based his decision. He asked for a specific response with a specific time. He even promised his reader a benefit: repeat sales.

WHOM TO CC

The "cc" (carbon copy) line is your chance to let the boss know what you're doing. On your "To" line you list the readers who are most directly affected by your memo. These are the people who will be following up with you on the project.

On your "cc" line you list the people who are not directly affected by the memo's contents but whom you'd like to keep "in the loop."

The letters "cc" are lowercase, and the information is generally placed at the bottom of the last page of the memo.

List the "cc" recipients in descending order of corporate hierarchy or in alphabetical order (as in the "To" line). Since the "cc" line often has as much political function as purposeful function, consider more strongly using the hierarchical order here.

A refinement of the "cc" function is the "bcc": blind carbon copy. This information is placed directly below the "cc" list, but only on the copy that is routed to the "bcc" name. Hence your other readers of the memo, those listed in the "To" line or at the "cc" line, do not realize the "bcc" reader has been routed the memo. The political charge that runs through all office memos is here laid naked.

Thirteen

FAXES

"Can you fax that to me?"

If you're like me, you both love and hate that question. You love it if you're asking it. You hate the question if you're on the receiving end. Faxes seem to disrupt the office routine just enough to make you mutter about the extra minutes' work the fax machine takes to save the extra days' waiting on the mail.

Generally, the desired information in your fax is a survey or a report or chart or some sort of already–written piece of work: Your fresh ideas or comments are subsidiary to its attachment. If your jotted thoughts were what your faxee wanted, he probably could have simply asked you for them over the phone, when instead he asked you to fax him something. This type of accompaniment fax memo is therefore simple.

In the spirit of the fact that a business letter or memo should always "cut to the chase," and that this just-the-facts-ma'am spirit is heightened when a fax is called for, keep it short and sweet.

COVER PAGE?

The most common way to address and introduce a fax is with a cover sheet. Generally this page is set up much like a memo page, except that it's headed FAX rather than MEMO, and usually there's a fill-in-the-blank for the number of pages sent.

Do you always need to use a cover sheet? Unless you know your recipient well and know just how she'll use the information, I suggest one. You might be surprised how often faxed information is saved and shared. A no-longer-pertinent note scrawled atop a document is distracting. Do your recipient the favor of letting her present the information you've faxed in a way that allows her the greatest professionalism. That means no distraction of faxed-on notes.

But if you've got a "fax relationship" with someone to whom you regularly fax a single page of one-shot information—go ahead, drop the formality of a cover page. It probably rarely says anything beyond "Here ya go," anyway. And if the page you're faxing has a "hole" where you can write without obscuring the faxed information, jot your message there. Just write big (and thick) enough that your recipient's name is legible.

Stick-on notes are available that bear the traditional To/From/Pages fill-in-the-blanks. These look a bit more professional than a hand-scrawled note, though I feel the machinelike look of a fax benefits from the personal touch of a human-scripted intro. The stick-on notes work well to draw the recipient's eye to your message, though. Again, as long as the note doesn't cover up necessary information, feel free to use these.

COVER PAGE!

But *most* of the time you'll want to use a cover page. The key note here, again, is brevity. Handwritten notes are perfectly acceptable as long as your writing is sufficiently legible, though I would consider typing out any note of more than about three or four sentences. You'll be surprised how a note whose text takes only fifteen square inches or so of type sprawls on and on when handwritten. Also, typing reduces the odds that one of your handwritten words or numbers will be illegible to your recipient—a likelihood that increases as the number of words you handwrite rises.

Make sure your cover letter bears *your* phone number and fax number. This eases fixing two fax mistakes: If you send the document to the wrong fax number (a rare but real concern) or if some part or some page of your transmission doesn't come through (a common problem).

Date the fax, of course. Address your fax using your recipient's first and last name. Include his title or department if he works in a large office. A fax machine is often shared by a large number of employees, and a fax simply addressed to Bob will readily be mislaid.

Fill in the blank that describes the number of pages you're sending. Fax technology is still raw: Missing pages are a common cause of confusion (and much refaxing).

Tell the recipient no more than he needs to know. "As you requested" is a perfectly acceptable fax cover sheet message, for instance.

If you're supplying more information that that, a fax message basically mimics the memo form. A "Subject" line is appropriate. Bullets and numbered points are fine, too. If you insist on finding style differences between mailed memos and faxed memos, faxes can probably bear a bit more telegraphic style than is appropriate for a hard-copy memo.

Though faxed memos are a bit more likely to be read and directly thrown away, a great many faxes are filed and later referenced, just like standard memos. Keep your information to a minimum, but don't fall into the trap of shooting off impenetrable-tomorrow messages such as, ''Yes, I can. Please send me one as soon as possible.'' This type of message is rarely a time-saver in the long run.

And don't forget, *anybody* is likely is read that fax between the time it spits out of the roller and the time it hits your recipient's in-box. Say nothing you don't want shared around that office.

Don't forget to sign the fax memo—just an initial will do to inject at least a modicum of humanity into an otherwise machine-slick piece of paper.

Fourteen

ELECTRONIC MAIL

Electronic mail—E-mail—enables a computer user to send a message that appears on another computer user's screen. It's simply a system for sending an on-screen memo. You can't send E-mail to anyone who simply has a computer, of course. The computers must be linked, networked. Most often this networking is limited to a single office site or building, but a growing number of companies are linking different offices—the Dallas office, say, with the New York and Los Angeles offices, and perhaps links to its suppliers.

E-mail has two great advantages: It's easy and it's instantaneous. Messages appear on one or more targeted screens immediately after sending.

E-mail has two great disadvantages: To know he has an E-mail memo, your recipient(s) must turn his computer on. Secondly, E-mail is a mite *too* easy. E-mail enthusiasts may overwhelm others with incessant chatter.

E-mail's usefulness is sending officewide "housekeeping" memos—the type you'll want to file and later refer to—is debatable. Most E-mail messages cannot be printed out and filed. Even if your system provides for this, why put each employee through the effort of printing out and distributing to himself his own memo? Just send around a paper memo, I say.

An E-mail system is found, not surprisingly, chiefly in businesses or departments in which many of the employees use a computer every day.

Not everyone turns on the computer every day. Unless you do, you won't know you have a message there.

But E-mail is a good way to get a computer user's attention. A memo sitting quietly in an in-box is easier to ignore than a blinking "MAIL" alert on your computer screen. Also E-mail breaks the "telephone tag" cycle.

Some companies seem to love using E-mail. Workers there are likely to find twelve or fifteen E-mail messages waiting each morning. At other companies, the sole E-mail many workers get is the occasional "Lunch, Joe?—Bob" note.

For E-mail fans, the link between finding a thought and finding the E-mail key seems annoyingly fused. Other people regard E-mail as too "techie" and vaguely déclassé; these people are probably unsure how to even send the darn things.

Most E-mail systems automatically display the message's origination time, its sender, and its distribution target (to "Bob," to "Payroll Department," to "All Employees").

I can only advise using E-mail the way your coworkers— and your bosses—do.

If you choose to send an E-mail message:

- Recognize that your reader will probably trash your message after reading it. If it's a message she'll want to write down, *you* consider writing it down *for* her by sending a paper memo.
- Keep it short. Don't annoy your reader by forcing him to page through a long E-mail message that offered him no forewarning of its intimidating length. And don't bump his other potential E-mail by taking all the storage space allotted.

E-mail should be a time-saver and an interruption-easer. Don't abuse the system.

E-MAIL AND PRIVACY

Because E-mail allows you to target your memo directly to a single person using a computer to which he probably punches in a personalized "access code," you may confuse E-mail with personal, behind-closed-doors conversation. Don't. E-mail sometimes goes astray; users swap computers and computer codes; and an office network manager can likely call up all the E-mail that travels her network—even after it's trashed. If you have something confidential to say, say it in person.

The laws regarding the privacy of E-mail have generally ruled that any messages are the property of the employer; your company has every right to read your E-mail.

Certain companies also insist that E-mail use is restricted only to company business—no personal use, please. If this is the policy, follow it.

E-MAIL AND THE HUMAN TOUCH

There's no gainsaying that many people find computers off-puttingly cold and "machine-y." These people will not welcome E-mail. If someone you know—a boss or coworker—views computers with vague distaste, you might consider phoning him rather than E-mailing him.

But E-mail also allows you to avoid the human touch with people you don't like or who don't like you.

Fifteen

WORKING WITH A SECRETARY

Do you type your own letters and memos, or does a secretary?

If you type them yourself—on a typewriter or a word processor—you're the boss. Typo? Awkwardness? Do it over, if you like. It's your time and it's your schedule that dictates when you get back the revised version.

If your secretary types them, you're his boss, but in a way he's your boss, too. True, his job generally is to help you do your job. If you ask him to retype a 16-page letter for the fifth time . . . well, that's what he's paid to do, right? And if you ask him to drop his complicated filing to retype a memo, when he's up to only "G" and will have to spend ten minutes to find where he left off . . . well, dammit, you need it *now*, don't you? Yes, but . . .

Few of us possess the callousness to assume our employees have no personal stake in their duties. Being a good manager includes keeping our workers and coworkers eager and involved. Unnecessary make-work, imperiously imposed, is bad management.

Aim for a collegial relationship that both letter writer and letter typist feel is efficient and productive.

DICTATION

Dictating routine correspondence is a great time-saver to the letter writer. Let's face it, most people can talk faster than even the fastest typist can keyboard, and certainly anyone can talk faster than he can write a letter by hand.

If you regularly dictate your letters, into a tape recorder or to a stenographer, you'll probably find a manner that works for you. Ask your secretary how it's working for her. Do you talk too quickly? Do you backtrack so incessantly that the typist spends more time erasing his typing than typing the words that stand? Find the method that helps you work as a team.

Focus on the letter or memo you're dictating; don't wander into conversation. Finish each thought before beginning another. If you're recording your letter, listen to it before you send it on for typing. Erase and start over if you're wholly dissatisfied.

If you find it difficult to form your thoughts in front of a stenographer, or if you freeze up at the tape recorder, try writing out your first draft. Then read it out as dictation. With practice, you may find this step unnecessary. Or you may find this read-from-outline approach your most efficient method of working.

KEEP DRAFTS DOWN

Nobody likes doing something over and over. You don't and your secretary doesn't. How can we go from getting the idea for a letter to its mailing with the fewest number of retakes?

Let's look first at the secretary's obligations. He must provide the letter sender with a typo-free, professionally laid-out letter or memo that reflects a reasonable interpretation of the sender's dictated words or written draft. Few people would argue the first two obligations: A properly typed, properly spaced letter or memo is the heart and sum of many secretaries' chief function. But how much "interpretation" can you expect of your secretary? It depends on the team you two forge over time. But it's the rare, lucky letter writer who can depend on her secretary to clean up her grammar and tidy her sometimes-spooling thoughts. An even more precious bit of teamwork is that of a secretary who spots her boss's substantive mistakes. This gift is a boon; it's not an expectation. If the two of you share this facility, bind that secretary to you with hoops of steel.

The executive's responsibility is to provide his secretary letter- or memo-making material that is as unambiguous and in as near-final form as possible. Lengthy letters or memos must often go through more than one draft; that's reasonable. But if even the simplest three-paragraph letter is taking you three or more drafts . . . you or your secretary is doing something wrong.

Think clearly. Speak clearly. Pencil your edits clearly. Notice where mistakes are made and spend a little extra time *before* you aim at your final draft. In the end, this extra effort should save you time and annoyance.

Letters that must be fully retyped to incorporate corrections offer the greatest opportunity for redraft problems, of course. A word processor's facility with redrafts is probably the tool's greatest gift to a secretary. Corrections can be made with little risk of introducing new errors. The risk of frazzled retype nerves is lessened, too. But sent through the typewriter . . . well, we've all probably known typists who can never correct a typo without introducing two more.

AH, LET IT GO?

When should you "let it go," despite a letter or memo's noted imperfection? Each circumstance is different. However, most businesspeople would agree that a professionally typed business letter of one or two pages—on letterhead and with all the trappings of officialness—should never go into the mail with conscious typos or handwritten corrections. Unreasonably or not, such bits of human imperfection look sloppy and amateurish to most business professionals.

Some would argue a handwritten postscript (a P.S.) is acceptable; some savants go so far as to claim it adds a desirable personal touch to a typewritten letter. But I maintain a postscript instead throws doubt on the organization of your thoughts in general.

Sending a letter back for retyping because it is spaced awkwardly is an even tougher call. After all, a typo is undeniably "wrong." But rejecting a letter because it hugs only the top third of a page or because it squeezes the closing and the signature line is more a matter of taste than of science. Still, remember what we said in an earlier chapter: That business letter represents you. An awkward-looking letter is the paper equivalent of a misbuttoned shirt or uncombed hair. Would you enter a meeting that way?

Sixteen

WORKING WITH WORD PROCESSORS

Throughout this book I've sung the praises of word processors and computers. Anyone who has written with these machines would agree that they vastly simplify and speed up writing, editing, and the production of a printed page.

I use the terms computer and word processor interchangeably, though in theory they vary. A computer is the hardware—the keyboard, monitor, and CPU (central processing unit, the box with disks and drives and whirs and gizmos). A word processor is really the software—the program that tells the machine what to do when you hit the keys.

For a short while, typewriters in some offices were replaced by dedicated word processors. These weren't computers in the usual sense in that operators couldn't readily change the program. They were like "smart" typewriters. This trend was short-lived, as computer prices fell and the valuable flexibility of "true" computers was recognized.

Most offices that produce any volume of mail at all now generally have computers available to all secretaries—if not one at each desk, then one for each small group. Many executives, too, have grown to depend on having a computer on their desks to make work easier—often to track sales calls, run spreadsheets, *and* write letters and memos.

POPULAR CHOICES

Most often, your choice of computer—both hardware and software—is made for you by your office manager. It's to your advantage to use the same system everyone else does. This enables you or your secretary to readily use someone else's equipment if yours goes down, and eases your use of a coworker's information on disk.

The two chief hardware families are the IBM-compatible and the Apple families. The IBM system probably has wider acceptance among U.S. offices; the Apple system (Macintosh is its current office-desk standard-bearer) is generally considered easier to learn and use.

The two most popular word processing programs are Microsoft Word (from Microsoft Inc.) and WordPerfect (from WordPerfect Corp.), available for both the IBM-type and Apple systems. MacWrite (Claris Corp.) is a highly popular Apple-only program. These programs all work well. Given the choice, choose to learn one of the popular programs—you increase the odds you won't have to learn a new program if you move to a new job.

Printers are often the weak link in the computer correspondence chain. A good printer produces smooth characters that look just as polished as any typewriter's. You certainly need not settle for the jerky, dot-comprised sort that long made computer-generated letters unwelcome. A laser printer (expensive) or ink-jet printer (less so) produce letter-quality or quite acceptable near-letter-quality characters. They're quiet, though not always fast. A dot-matrix printer is fast but noisy; most dot-matrix printers do not generate pleasingly smooth characters.

What You Can Do

With a computer, you can:

- Edit words and phrases quickly and easily
- Change the order of paragraphs
- Painlessly shift a letter up or down on the page
- Check your spelling automatically
- Store frequently used sentences or paragraphs for one-key insertion
- Look good

A computer is a tool that eases getting your thoughts out of your head and onto paper. It encourages you to experiment and to fine-tune the bits of the experiment that work.

Writing good business letters and memos is sometimes fun; it's often painful. It should always be rewarding.

If you enjoyed this No Nonsense Guide you may want to order these other No Nonsense Guides: